Genesis to Revelation

Genesis to Revelation

365 Daily Devotions

C L WHITEWAY

ISBN: 9798862180534

ACKNOWLEDGEMENTS

All thanks and praise, first and foremost, to God - for giving me the task of completing such a devotional and for directing me in what to write.

I would also like to thank my Mum, who sadly never got to see the finished work - for all her love, encouragement, and support - especially during the early years and during the tough moments – thank you Mum!

Thanks also go to my friend Lyn who has helped with the task of proof-reading the devotional, along with David Hall.

Without the help and encouragement of my brother this devotional would never have made it into print – thank you bro for all your hard work!

And finally, thanks to my long-suffering husband, Les - for putting up with me through all my 'ups' and 'downs' as I have worked on the book through the years!

I couldn't have done it without you all.

PREFACE

I have written this devotional, with God's help, with a love and passion to share God's Word - which reveals His heart of love for his people.

I do hope that you will join me on this journey - from 'Genesis' to 'Revelation' - and that it will inspire you to read more of God's Word.

I pray that, as you do so, - God will speak to you in a most personal and powerful way and that as a result your faith will be strengthened, your joy renewed and your heart filled with His peace.

May you taste and see that the Lord is good!

01 JANUARY

Let's Start at the Very Beginning

Genesis 1 v 1: In the beginning God…

What better place to start at the beginning of this New Year than with the words – 'In the beginning – God.' Let's just pause for a moment and really think about that. Before this world ever began, there was God - he is and was before all things!

O how we would benefit in our lives if we focused on God first rather than on other things. But all too often we focus on our problems first and then wonder why we are in such a mess - becoming all stressed out trying to solve them. And yet, if only in the beginning we focused on God, how much better our days would go and how quickly we would find things falling into place.

So, at the start of this New Year, let's decide to put God first in our thoughts as we begin each day, and then see how differently each day turns out as a result.

O Father, forgive me for the times when you are the last person I think about during the day. Please help me to put you first – right at the beginning of my day. Amen.

1

02 JANUARY

No Spirit, No Life

Genesis 1 v 2: Now the earth was formless and empty, darkness was over the surface of the deep, and the Spirit of God was hovering over the waters.

Before God began speaking creation into being – the Holy Spirit was there – hovering, just waiting to get to work and bring life into this desolate place.

Does your life feel formless, empty and dark right now? If so, take heart – for the same Spirit that hovered over those ancient waters is hovering over you! Yes, right at this very moment, God's Spirit is waiting to come in and transform your life! He longs to fill you to overflowing with all that He is! Will you invite him in?

If this is you today, then please take this opportunity to ask the Holy Spirit to fill you and have his way in your life.

I admit Lord, that my life does feel rather formless, empty and dark right now. Thank you for your Spirit that is hovering over me, longing to give me life in all its fullness. I ask Him to come in now, and do the work that only He can do in me - in Jesus' name. Amen.

03 JANUARY

We Need One Another

Genesis 2 v 18: The LORD God said, "It is not good for the man to be alone."

We were all made for relationships and these relationships matter to God – for they were His idea in the first place; but do we sometimes take them for granted?

God himself says, it's not good to be alone, and yet lots of people are very lonely and isolated in our society today. I wonder - are there any ways in which we can help? Maybe there is someone who is lonely living near you? Maybe they would appreciate a visit or a phone call?

It is quite possible to feel alone in a crowd and even within a marriage! O how we need Jesus!

Thank you Father that you value relationships and that they are part of your plan for our lives. Help me to first and foremost value my relationship with You, but at the same time, not forget those who may need some companionship and love. May I not take those who love me for granted, and I thank you that you are always with me! Amen.

3

04 JANUARY

No Use Hiding

Genesis 3 v 10: He answered, "I heard you in the garden, and I was afraid because I was naked; so I hid."

There will always be feelings of guilt, fear and shame arising within us whenever we disobey God. As a result the relationship between us becomes strained, just as it does in any human relationship, until we confess our misdeeds to God and receive his forgiveness.

Instead of running away from God and hiding, which is our natural tendency, we need to be immediate in coming to him and ask for his forgiveness, believing that he loves us and is more than ready to forgive. Our God is slow to anger, quick to forgive and abounding in love.

I know I often fail you Lord, and when I do, I feel you are angry and far away; but the TRUTH is – you are right here longing for me to turn to You and ask for your forgiveness. Help me to be eager to do this Lord, so that our relationship may be quickly restored. Amen.

05 JANUARY

Family Matters

Genesis 7 v 1: The LORD then said to Noah, "Go into the ark, you and your whole family, because I have found you righteous in this generation."

In case you didn't already know - your family matters to God. As we can see from this verse today, only Noah is said to have been righteous, but his whole family are told to go into the ark with him and are saved from the flood.

Yes, God cares about families. For example - Lot's family would all have been saved had they followed the angels' instructions (see Genesis 19 v 12 - 33). Rahab, after she had hidden the spies, was told her life would be spared along with her entire family (see Joshua 6 v 17). Cornelius had all his family and friends come to hear Peter's message and they were all filled with the Holy Spirit (see Acts 10 v 24 & 44). And the Philippian Jailer's whole family was saved and baptised along with him (see Acts 16 v 31 – 34). So don't ever give up praying for your loved ones' salvation!

I place my whole family into your hands Lord, knowing that you love them and long to save them. May I be faithful in praying for those that don't yet know you, and I look forward to the day when they do! Amen.

06 JANUARY

Is He Calling You?

Genesis 12 v 1: The LORD had said to Abram, "Leave your country, your people and your father's household and go to the land I will show you."

Are you being called to leave something behind and to step out in faith – one step at a time, as God leads you? Are you holding back through fear of the unknown, what people may think, or fear of failure maybe?

God is faithful; he will not call you without helping you and providing for you - every step of the way. So put your hand in His and trust Him to lead and guide you into all that He has for you.

O Father please help me, I have heard you calling me but I am frightened to let go of all that is familiar and comfortable. Please give me the strength and courage that I need to finally let go and to put ALL my trust in You as I launch out into the unknown. Amen.

07 JANUARY

Any Clever Ideas?

Genesis 16 v 2: … so she said to Abram, "The LORD has kept me from having children. Go, sleep with my maidservant; perhaps I can build a family through her." Abram agreed to what Sarai said.

Have you ever tried to help God out? So often we get impatient waiting for him to come through on a promise he has made us. So we get restless and start to come up with some of our own 'clever' ideas – just to help things along!

This is exactly what happened to Sarai, Abram's wife. In not having faith that God would enable her to bear a child in old age, she came up with her own plan and managed to talk her husband into it as well! A BIG mistake!

Forgive me Father when I try to take things into my own hands; when I climb into the driver's seat and think I know best; daring to think that my plan will work out better that yours ever could. How could I be so arrogant Lord when you Always know what's best? Please forgive me. Amen.

08 JANUARY

Don't Look Back

Genesis 19 v 26: But Lot's wife looked back, and she became a pillar of salt.

Lot and his family had been told not to look back as they fled from Sodom and Gomorrah, but Lot's wife just couldn't resist that inner pull, just to see what had happened. Had it all really gone? - her lovely home? - all of her belongings? - her old way of life?

How often do we do a similar thing? We start off following our Lord, but as we set off do we think about what we've left behind and long to turn back?

Jesus said that anyone who puts his hand to the plough and looks back is not fit for service in the kingdom of God. Elisha, when called to follow Elijah, did go back – but only to burn up his livelihood and say goodbye to his family: in other words to make a clean break with his past (see 1 Kings 19 v 19 – 21).

O Father, forgive me for any tendency I have to look backwards instead of forward to where you are leading me. Help me today, to make the decision to let go of the past and wholeheartedly follow you – no turning back! Amen.

09 JANUARY

Do You Have an Isaac?

Genesis 22 v 12: "Do not lay a hand on the boy," he said. "Do not do anything to him. Now I know that you fear God because you have not withheld from me your son, your only son."

God may often 'test' us – but he will not push us beyond what he knows we can bear. He wants us to become aware of the true state of our heart towards him. We may not be aware when we have let other things crowd in and take his place.

Whenever God asks us to give up anything it is always for our good, for he only wants what is best for us in the long term.

Do you have an Isaac? Something or someone you'd find difficult to sacrifice? It isn't easy – but we need to love God more than anything else, for that is His desire and what he so rightly deserves.

O Lord I confess, my heart shudders at the very thought of being in Abraham's shoes. Could I really go through with it, if you asked of me a similar thing? Help me love you first Lord; let no 'idol' come between us. Amen.

10 JANUARY

He Goes Before You

Genesis 24 v 14: May it be that when I say to a girl, 'Please let down your jar that I may have a drink,' and she says, 'Drink, and I'll water your camels too' – let her be the one you have chosen for your servant Isaac.

This story, in Genesis chapter 24, has always warmed my heart, as it shows us how the Lord can lead and guide us into his perfect will, IF we will allow him to. I love how the Lord answers the servant's prayer before he's even finished praying, and a silent prayer at that (see v 15). The Lord even led him to pray the right words – so that he was guaranteed the right result!

Earlier, he was told that God would send his angel ahead of him so that he would have success (see v 7). God had indeed gone before him in every way; and he will go before you in every way too!

Why not read the whole of the chapter next time you have a spare moment. I promise you, it will be well worth the effort!

How I thank you Lord, that I too can be guided by you in such an amazing way! Help me to always pray expectantly. Amen.

11 JANUARY

Before You Were Born

Genesis 25 v 22: The babies jostled each other within her, and she said, "Why is this happening to me?" So she went to enquire of the LORD.

God knows ALL things. Before we were born God knew us entirely - what a thought! He knew about us way before our parents ever did! He is indeed our TRUE Father!

Rebekah had two future nations within her, and they were already fighting! Before her boys were born, God saw them and understood them!

The unborn child is seen as just as important to God as the child that has been born. We can see this illustrated when John the Baptist leapt while still inside his mother's womb - when Mary arrived and greeted his mother, Elizabeth (see Luke 1 v 41).

O Father, it just amazes me when I realise that you knew everything about me before I was born - that I mattered to you just as much while I was still in my mother's womb as I do right now! Thank you Father. Amen.

12 JANUARY

I Had a Dream

Genesis 37 v 5: Joseph had a dream, and when he told it to his brothers, they hated him all the more.

When you or I have a 'dream' - a vision, a goal – not everyone is going to be happy for us, and we should expect this and accept it.

Without a vision, the people perish. Dreams are good; we all need to have a vision and goal for our future, even if it's a long way off and seems impossible right now. Don't let go of your God-given dreams - they will come to pass!

If you don't have a dream right now – then ask God to give you one. Ask him what it is he wants you to do. If you seek him with all your heart - he will show you - in His time.

Thank you Lord for giving us dreams – please give me a vision for my future; and may I trust you with its fulfilment, however long it takes. Amen.

13 JANUARY

Flee Temptation!

Genesis 39 v 12: She caught him by his cloak and said, "Come to bed with me!" But he left his cloak in her hand and ran out of the house.

Whenever you are faced with temptation and feel there's no way out – remember this. You can always turn away and run in the opposite direction. Or you can choose to change your thoughts and focus on something else. Or you can decide not to let those hurtful words come out of your mouth, simply by keeping it closed. We are never quite as helpless as we make out.

Next time, and there will be a next time, you find yourself up against it – think of what Joseph did and ask God to show you your best method of escape!

Thank you Lord, you have promised to provide me with a way out whenever I am tempted. Please help me to find the way and to follow it. Amen.

14 JANUARY

Treasures in the Darkness

Genesis 39 v 20-21: ... But while Joseph was there in the prison, the LORD was with him; he showed him kindness and granted him favour in the eyes of the prison warder.

Maybe you are in a 'prison' right now; where things don't make any sense and you wonder, 'where is God in all of this?' Well, He is right there, in the middle of the mess, with you!

He is longing to comfort and help you through this dark and distressing situation. He will bring you through it and out the other side. Know that He is for you and does have a purpose to work out through this – even though you may not see it now. Remember, diamonds are formed in the dark and under pressure!

Never let me forget Lord that you are with me – even in the darkest times of my life. You will never leave me or forsake me; for that I am truly grateful. Amen.

15 JANUARY

What a Difference a Day Makes

Genesis 41 v 14: So Pharaoh sent for Joseph, and he was quickly brought from the dungeon.

When Joseph woke up that morning, it was just like any other he'd woken up to since he'd been put in prison. He had no idea what was about to happen to him – how his life was about to change completely - and the same can be true for you!

Suddenly there is a call and he is ushered out of his dungeon and into Pharaoh's presence, never to return to his prison again! Not only was he set free that day, but he was also made the most powerful man in all Egypt, apart from Pharaoh himself. Wow, can you imagine how that felt?

So be encouraged - never lose hope when you are going through tough times or are in dark places, because you never know when it could suddenly all change!

O Lord, please help me to hold on to the hope that you will come to my rescue, and that it will be at just the right time. Thank you Lord! Amen.

16 JANUARY

Evil Turned Into Good

Genesis 50 v 20: You intended to harm me, but God intended it for good to accomplish what is now being done, the saving of many lives.

This verse is one of my favourites; it just amazes me that God can use our wickedness to bring about his own good purposes! Not that this should give us an excuse to behave badly; far from it! But rather, how we should marvel at God's sovereignty over all things! There is nothing God cannot do and he certainly knows how to turn things around and make all things work together for good for those who love him!

Knowing this should set us free from any doubts or fears we may have. For even if we get it wrong and make a mistake, God isn't surprised by it and he already has the plan of how to turn it all into good!

How can I thank you enough for your sovereignty? I am in awe of your works O Lord; I stand amazed! Thank you for saving me from myself – from those things I know I shouldn't do. Thank you that even my weaknesses can be turned into your opportunities. Amen.

17 JANUARY

The Fear of God

Exodus 1 v 17: The midwives, however, feared God and did not do what the king of Egypt had told them to do; they let the boys live.

We don't hear much about the fear of God these days, as the fear of man has very much taken over, through both social and political pressure.

These midwives, however, knew what it meant to fear God and as a result they were blessed with families of their own (see verse 21).

I wonder - are there any areas in your life where you are allowing the fear of man to control you, rather than the fear of God? It's worth taking some time to think about. Are we more interested in pleasing people when, in fact, first and foremost we should be pleasing God?

O Lord, how have we managed to lose sight of that reverential fear of You? Please forgive us and bring to our minds any situations in which we fear man over and above you and help us to stop! Amen.

18 JANUARY

Let Go and Let God

Exodus 2 v 3: But when she could hide him no longer, she got a papyrus basket for him and coated it with tar and pitch. Then she placed the child in it and put it among the reeds along the bank of the Nile.

What amazing faith Moses' mother had, to leave her baby son on the edge of the Nile – not knowing what would happen to him! She had to 'let go' and totally trust God with the outcome - she could do no more.

Am I speaking to someone today who really needs to do the same? You have done all you can and God is now asking you to hand it all over to Him, and for you to fully let go! It's frightening - yes - to place everything you've been nurturing totally into God's hands. It's that final letting go that's so hard isn't it? But it will be worth it – for it can be in no better place, than in God's care.

O Father, please give me the strength and courage I need to finally let go. I have done all I can and I now place everything in your hands – trusting you with the outcome. Amen.

18

19 JANUARY

Oh No, Not Me!

Exodus 4 v 13: But Moses said, "O Lord, please send someone else to do it."

Have you ever found yourself saying this very same thing to God? Well it's exactly what Moses said when he was told to go and speak to Pharaoh. Even after God assured him that He would be with him, had given him various signs to perform and promised to help him speak well – Moses still didn't want to do it. In fact it wasn't until God got angry and said his brother could go with him and be his mouthpiece, that Moses finally agreed to go!

Moses had questioned God and had come up with reasons why it wouldn't work and why he wasn't right for the job. Sound familiar? But God had specifically chosen him and he has specifically chosen you too! So quit fighting it and let God use you as he wants to.

O Father, please forgive me for the times I wriggle and squirm and try to get out of something I know You are asking me to do. If You are asking me to do it then You will give me all I need to accomplish it. Help me to truly believe this.
Amen.

20 JANUARY

Hard to Believe

Exodus 6 v 9: Moses reported this to the Israelites, but they did not listen to him because of their discouragement and cruel bondage.

Moses had told the Israelites that, despite the fact that things had just got worse, God was still on their side and was going to bring them out from under the yoke of the Egyptians and take them into the land he had promised them. But they just couldn't take it on board as they were so downhearted.

After being knocked down for so long and in so many ways, it can be hard to really believe in a good report. Our feelings tend to rule us, and therefore deprive us of the very 'hope' that we so desperately need.

The Lord understands this.

Thank you Lord for understanding my heart; when it's feeling so discouraged that it cannot take in anything good. But please help me to stand on your good promises, despite how I may be feeling, for therein lies my true 'hope'. Amen.

21 JANUARY

Shed Your Light Lord

Exodus 10 v 23: No-one could see anyone else or leave his place for three days. Yet all the Israelites had light in the places where they lived.

The plague of 'darkness' brought about a great distinction between the Egyptians and the Israelites; without the 'light' the Egyptians were paralysed – they couldn't go anywhere, whereas the Israelites, who had the light - could!

As this is true physically, so it is also true spiritually; for without the light of the Lord we cannot see where we are going and so become paralysed – we cannot move forward. O how we need the Lord's light to guide us and show us the way ahead!

In the darkness the Egyptians also couldn't see one another, and we have similar problems with relationships when we leave the Lord outside them.

O Lord, how I need your 'light', and especially the light from your Word, to lead and guide me in everything, so I can function properly as you intended. Amen.

22 JANUARY

Give Yourself a Break!

Exodus 12 v 16: ... Do no work at all on these days, except to prepare food for everyone to eat – that is all you may do.

God wanted his people to rest while they celebrated the feast of Passover, and he still wants us to rest today.

Work is important, yes, but equally important are the times of rest. We need to take time out, to relax and switch off from our busy lives, and time to recharge our batteries. There are many dangers to our health and well-being if we fail to take time off from work.

Many people find they feel guilty and can't relax when they stop working and only feel truly good about themselves when they are working. But God doesn't want us to gain our worth and value from what we do – he wants us to gain it from being loved by Him!

When we do take some time out to relax, it is good to think of all God has done for us and to thank and praise Him!

Please help me Father to take a break from my everyday activities, whatever they may be, and to rest in your love for me, knowing it's what you want me to do. Amen.

23 JANUARY

God Knows Best

Exodus 13 v 17: When Pharaoh let the people go, God did not lead them on the road through the Philistine country, though that was shorter. For God said, "If they face war, they might change their minds and return to Egypt."

Have you ever questioned the way God has taken you? Has it seemed illogical to your own understanding? Well this verse today shows us that God can see ahead and knows how we are going to react, and so he chooses the path that is best for us.

God could see that the Israelites weren't ready to face war and that if they did, they would most likely flee straight back to Egypt, the very place from which He had just delivered them!

Next time the Lord appears to be working against your plan, realise that he knows what he's doing and has your very best interests at heart – even if it doesn't appear that way. If you are in this position today, then hand it all over to God and trust Him – for He knows best!

I thank you Lord that you know exactly what I can handle and I trust you to lead me in the way that's best for me. May I be obedient and follow you. Amen.

24 JANUARY

No Way!

Exodus 14 v 14: The LORD will fight for you; you need only to be still.

At times in our life we will see no way out of a situation. We have tried to work out a solution - a way of escape – but nothing seems to work. We may even have been led into this predicament by the Lord himself! So what is he saying to us?

When the Israelites were trapped – caught between the Egyptians and the Red Sea – they saw no way of escape as there was literally nowhere to run or hide. But God came through for them at the last minute in the most amazing way, a way they could never have imagined, for He made a way where there was no way!

I wonder, am I speaking to someone today who really has their back up against the wall and you can see no way out of your difficulty? Well take heart, and believe in God for he is able to deliver you out of that hopeless situation. For with God there is always a way!

O Lord, how I need your help! I give up all my efforts and ask you to deliver me. I trust you Lord! Amen.

25 JANUARY

Awesome!

Exodus 15 v 11: Who among the gods is like you, O LORD? Who is like you – majestic in holiness, awesome in glory, working wonders?

Have you lost your sense of 'awe' of God? Has he become so familiar to you that you've almost brought him down to your level? Have you forgotten that he's a holy and majestic God? Have you forgotten his Power? It can be easy to lose sight of just how 'Awesome' our God is.

Take a really close look at anything God has created and it will soon fill you with both awe and wonder! It's not that we worship creation itself, but rather that creation reveals just how AMAZING God is!

Of course God could part the Red Sea, for he had commanded it into existence in the first place. Spend some time today thinking about just how GREAT your God is!

Sadly, I am ashamed to say, I have lost my sense of awe and wonder of you Lord. Please forgive me for bringing you down to my level and restore that sense of awe of you, deep in my heart; for You truly are an AWESOME God! Amen.

26 JANUARY

Food for Thought

Exodus 16 v 12: I have heard the grumbling of the Israelites. Tell them, 'At twilight you will eat meat, and in the morning you will be filled with bread. Then you will know that I am the LORD your God.'

God has our number – he hears every complaint we make against him; for whenever we complain, it is ultimately against Him!

How loving is our God that he should bear with us, with all our complaining, and bless us by supplying our needs. Not only were the Israelites fed from heaven itself, they were also forgiven for their complaining. Now that certainly is food for thought!

If you have a tendency to murmur, grumble or complain, then turn away from it now; for it hurts God far more than you could know!

O Father I am brought face to face with my sin today. Please forgive me for all my complaining; I didn't realise it was You I was angry with; I didn't realise it was You I was hurting. Please cleanse me from this sin Lord and help me to speak only positive words. Amen.

27 JANUARY

Doing Too Much?

Exodus 18 v 17: Moses' father-in-law replied, "What you are doing is not good."

Moses is sitting as the only judge for all the people, and is therefore kept very busy – too busy in fact! Does that sound like anyone you know?

Look at what Moses' father-in-law says – 'What you are doing is not good!' If someone said that to us, we might think they were being rather negative and possibly even inspired by the devil. But how wrong we would be – for these words from Jethro were, in fact, full of Godly wisdom.

Maybe the work you are doing is 'good' in itself, but if you are working all the time, so that you have no spare time for anything or anyone else, then it is not good! Maybe today would be a good day to take a proper look at all you are doing and then prayerfully consider which things you should and shouldn't continue.

Please show me Lord if I need to cut out anything from my schedule or if there is someone else who would gladly take on a role. May I not assume that I am the only one that can do it. Thank you Lord. Amen.

28 JANUARY

Come Up Higher

Exodus 19 v 20: The LORD descended to the top of Mount Sinai and called Moses to the top of the mountain. So Moses went up...

Is the Lord calling you to come up higher? In order for Moses to meet with God he had to leave the people at the foot of the mountain and had to climb up in obedience to God's call. Once at the top he was able to receive all that God had for him and for the people below!

I wonder - is this speaking to you? Are you being called to come up higher in your spiritual walk? Are you longing to receive all that God has for you? Are you willing to be obedient to that call and leave the crowd and go it alone for a time? God wants to have that close fellowship with you and as he pours out his heart to you, in turn you can go back down the mountain and share His heart with others Are you ready and willing to do just that?

It can be hard Lord, to come up higher – I feel so inadequate for the journey. I'll need to let go of a few things and a few people - but I want to do your will Lord. Please help me to come up to that higher place with you. Yes, I want to enjoy sweet fellowship with you. Amen.

29 JANUARY

Blatant Idolatry

Exodus 32 v 1: ... Come, make us gods who will go before us. As for this fellow Moses who brought us up out of Egypt, we don't know what has happened to him.

How quickly our thoughts and emotions can change and get in the way, leading us astray. One minute the Israelites were promising to keep God's commandments and the next they are blatantly disregarding them, by wanting an idol. Moses has now become 'this fellow' and their deliverance from Egypt is solely attributed to him. There is no mention of God having been involved at all! God has been airbrushed completely out of the story!

How quickly do we turn to other things for comfort when we don't perceive God as being there for us, even though he always is? Have we allowed so many idols into our lives that we can no longer see God's hand in our story? It is worth asking ourselves these questions when there is so much in today's society to distract us and lure us away from our God.

O Father, please forgive me for the times I turn to other things for comfort and help. Also for the times I forget you and leave you out of my life, and forget all that you have done for me. I am truly sorry Lord. Amen.

30 JANUARY

Gifted

Exodus 35 v 30-31: … See, the LORD has chosen Bezalel…
and he has filled him with the Spirit of God, with skill, ability
and knowledge in all kinds of crafts…

We need to forgive ourselves for thinking that the Holy
Spirit only equips us with 'spiritual' gifts – for his anointing is
far more outreaching than that; in fact it encompasses every
area of gifting. Here we have a man who is gifted directly by
the Spirit to carry out all the intricate craftwork for the
tabernacle; he is also given the gift to teach others (see v 34).
There was no end to his talent in craftsmanship; if you read on
in the passage you will see!

Is there something God is calling you to do – but you feel
way too inadequate to fulfil it? Then ask God to fill you with
his Holy Spirit, to enable you to carry out the task he has pre-
arranged for you. Those God calls he equips!

Thank you Father that when you ask me to do something I
cannot do naturally, I need not worry, as You are able to fill
me with your Holy Spirit and enable me. Help me remember
to ask for that infilling when I cannot do what lies before me.
Fill me now, in Jesus' name. Amen.

31 JANUARY

Divine Guidance

Exodus 40 v 36-37: In all the travels of the Israelites, whenever the cloud lifted from above the tabernacle, they would set out; but if the cloud did not lift, they did not set out until the day it lifted.

Unless the Lord went before them, the Israelites didn't move and so they had the assurance of always being in the right place - exactly where God wanted them! If only it was as easy for us.

Have you ever stepped out into something and suddenly realised that you were completely on your own and out of your depth? That in your excitement you completely left God out of the equation? Have you forgotten to take your lead from Him? It can be disastrous when we run ahead of God!

Or is God telling you to move on and you are staying firmly put and therefore missing out on all He has for you up ahead?

O Lord, we can learn so much from the Israelites and their obedience to follow you. Please let us know when to stay and when to go; let us always be guided by You. Then we will know we are exactly where you have placed us. Amen.

01 FEBRUARY

Keep on Burning

Leviticus 6 v 13: The fire must be kept burning on the altar continuously; it must not go out.

With a fire continually burning, the altar is always ready for the next sacrifice at any time of day or night.

God wants us to be available to Him 24/7! He may want to use us at any time and we need to be ready! We need to be open to what God is asking us to do – even if he wakes us in the middle of the night with a burden to pray for someone or some situation. For this is the true nature of sacrifice!

We need to keep on fire for Him, so that we are readily available for whatever he chooses to do through us. So the bottom line is - Don't let your fire go out!

O Lord, keep me alive and burning with passion for you. Please don't let my fire go out: may I always be available for you to use, however and whenever you choose; in Jesus' name. Amen.

02 FEBRUARY

Do as You're Told

Leviticus 9 v 6: Then Moses said, "This is what the LORD has commanded you to do, so that the glory of the LORD may appear to you."

The Lord asked the Israelites to bring Him various sacrifices and told them that 'today' the Lord would appear before them. They carried out everything just as he'd commanded, and as a result they all saw the glory of the Lord.

There is a lesson here for us. If we want to know more of God's presence in our lives, then we need to listen to what he's asking us to do and when we've heard, to obey in every detail. For God will always bless us for our obedience.

Maybe there's something God's asked you to do and you've been holding back? His Word for you today is, "Do what I've already told you - then my glory will be revealed to you!"

Doing what you ask of me Lord, will always bless me – I realise that now! Please help me to obey you straight away, rather than using delaying tactics. Thank you Lord for showing me this today. Amen.

03 FEBRUARY

Lost Reverence

Leviticus 19 v 30: Observe my Sabbaths and have reverence for my sanctuary. I am the LORD.

Sundays have fast become much like any other day of the week to most people, and church has become, in some instances, far less reverent. Have we lost our way to some degree in this generation? Have we been so influenced by this world's values that we've let them take over our Christian lives? It's a question I believe we need to seriously ask ourselves today.

Yes we want to be relevant, open to new ideas and ways to reach the lost, but not at the expense of losing our reverence and awe of God.

God once dwelt in His sanctuary, but now he dwells in each one of us who belong to Him. We therefore also need to show reverence to each other, for we are His sanctuary now!

*Forgive us Lord, for not taking your words about keeping Sundays as a 'special' day seriously enough, dedicated to You, and also for our lack of reverence towards both you, our Lord, and our brothers and sisters - who are the Church.
Amen.*

04 FEBRUARY

Be Holy

Leviticus 20 v 26: You are to be holy to me because I, the LORD, am holy, and I have set you apart from the nations to be my own.

What comes to mind when you hear the word holy? Someone who's 'holier than thou'? Some great saint who's wearing a halo perhaps? Someone who is perfect and never does anything wrong? Does it seem so far removed from the daily realities of your life that you could never attain to it?

The good news is – it is God Himself who is making us holy, for the initiative comes from Him, not us! He is the one who says we are to be holy and He is the one who has already set us apart. We just need to let Him have His way with us.

Also, did you notice? He wants us to be holy to Him, so we are like Him and set apart so that we can become His own. Yes, He wants us for Himself.

Help me realise Lord, that because you have set me apart for Yourself, I am being made holy by you; I just need to co-operate with all that you are doing in my life. Amen.

05 FEBRUARY

Feed the Poor

Leviticus 23 v 22: When you reap the harvest of your land, do not reap to the very edges of your field or gather the gleanings of your harvest. Leave them for the poor and the alien. I am the LORD your God.

What a wonderful provision God made for the poor; but they would only receive this blessing if God's words were obeyed.

It is in God's heart for us to take care of the poor, and we need to leave some of our blessings for them. We need to guard our hearts from wanting to keep everything to ourselves. We need to have generous hearts, like our Lord's. For when we 'give', we will be living as God intended - not just looking after number one, but thinking of others.

Love your neighbour, as you love yourself!

O Father, I confess, I tend to be so wrapped up in my own affairs and my own wants and needs that I often forget about other people and their genuine needs. Please instil in me a heart for those less fortunate than myself; may I be willing to 'give' as you do Lord. Amen.

06 FEBRUARY

Up Close and Personal

Leviticus 26 v 12: I will walk among you and be your God, and you will be my people.

God is not far away, as we so often imagine he is, but He is right here amongst us by His Spirit. His desire has always been to have a relationship with us. He wants to be involved in our everyday lives, and not just in the big things that concern us, but also in the small things that we might think He's too busy to be bothered with.

If you had a parent who wasn't really interested in who you were or what your interests were, then the chances are you may think your heavenly Father is the same - but He isn't! God wants to be close to you and involved in every area of your life. Isn't that amazing – the God who created the whole 'Universe' wants to be with YOU!

My heart is still reeling from this news Lord; that you care so much about me that you want to be close to me and are interested in everything that concerns me. I can't begin to thank you enough. Amen.

07 FEBRUARY

Break Every Chain

Leviticus 26 v 13: I am the LORD your God, who brought you out of Egypt so that you would no longer be slaves to the Egyptians; I broke the bars of your yoke and enabled you to walk with heads held high.

Do you feel the bars of heaviness bearing down upon you, from the burden you are carrying? Perhaps you find yourself gripped by addictions or bad habits that you just can't seem to shift. This is our present-day slavery – for we are slaves to whatever has mastered us!

But it need not be so, for God can intervene and set you free from every chain that binds you – but you must let Him have His way. If the Israelites had refused to leave Egypt, they would have remained in their slavery with their heads bowed low.

I encourage you, if this is you today – then cry out to God in prayer.

O God, you know all about me; you know exactly what's holding me down; those things I struggle with. I want to be set free Lord. I give you permission to break every chain, in Jesus' name. Amen.

08 FEBRUARY

Teamwork

Numbers 4 v 49: At the LORD's command through Moses, each was assigned his work and told what to carry.

If we were all carrying out the work the Lord had given us to do, then no one would be doing too much and no one too little. Each would be playing their rightful part, and as a result, the whole church would benefit.

There will be a greater sense of fellowship when we all pull together, rather than just a few people doing all the work. We will feel fulfilled when carrying out the tasks God has made especially for us, for he knows exactly what each one of us can carry.

Have you asked God how he would like you to serve Him within His church? Bear in mind, His guidance may well come through your church leaders.

O Heavenly Father, I so want to carry out the tasks that You have prepared for me. Help me let go of anything I shouldn't be doing right now, and I will gladly take on those things you are asking me to. Amen.

09 FEBRUARY

Confession is Good for the Soul

Numbers 5 v 6-7: ... When a man or woman wrongs another in any way and so is unfaithful to the LORD, that person is guilty and must confess the sin he has committed.

Yes, when we hurt others we are ultimately hurting God by being unfaithful to his commandments and therefore, we are guilty of sin.

God would like us to come clean with him and confess what we have done, rather than trying to cover it up and pretend it never happened. Suppressing things is not good for our health; it can often result in various ailments including depression. We were not created to harbour secrets.

Is there something you haven't confessed to the Lord? Well now is your opportunity to come clean with Him.

I am so sorry Lord, for the times I have hurt you by hurting others. Please forgive me for everything that you have brought to my mind today and help me to continue to keep a clean slate with you day by day. Thank you for your forgiveness. Amen.

10 FEBRUARY

What a Blessing!

Numbers 6 v 24-26: The LORD bless you and keep you; the LORD make his face shine upon you and be gracious to you; the LORD turn his face towards you and give you peace.

This blessing was given to the Israelites from God (via the priests), and is very much a window into God's heart for his people. It's such an amazing blessing that once received for yourself you can't help but want to pass it on to bless someone else!

May I suggest that you take time to fully absorb the words of this special blessing and then continue to meditate on them throughout the day; may you know for yourself God's deep and intimate care for you. Receive from Him today all that he wants to give you. Use this blessing to draw closer to God.

O Lord, I can't thank you enough for this wonderful blessing that reveals your true nature. Thank you Lord, for drawing me closer to you through it; may I in turn share it with others.
Amen.

11 FEBRUARY

Wait on the Lord

Numbers 9 v 8: Moses answered them, "Wait until I find out what the LORD commands concerning you."

What wise advice this was from Moses. He knew it would be foolish to try and come up with his own idea of what should be done in this situation, for what may have seemed good and right to him, may not have been the Lord's will. He didn't dare assume that he had the correct answer - not even in his God-ordained position as judge!

Are we in danger of rushing in to solve an issue before first consulting with our God? I think we quite easily fall into this trap, especially in this age of instant gratification! We often don't have the patience required to wait on the Lord. But if we want the right outcome, this is what we must do.

I confess Lord, how often I fail to seek Your guidance and rush in where fools fear to tread. Please help me to first bring everything to You in prayer. Amen.

12 FEBRUARY

Respect Your Leader

Numbers 12 v 1: Miriam and Aaron began to talk against Moses because of his Cushite wife, for he had married a Cushite.

Although Moses was their brother, this probably made them think they had some right to judge him. He was first and foremost their leader, and had been placed in authority over them by God. As their leader he should have been shown reverence and respect, but instead they are busy running him down behind his back – sound familiar?

This is a very big problem in society today, as there is so little respect for those in authority, we can easily forget how serious a sin this is in God's sight. Yes, even simply speaking words against your pastor is an abomination to God. We need to have our eyes opened to this and seriously need to repent.

I am so sorry for the times I have spoken out negative words about my pastors. Please forgive me Lord and help me to show love and support towards them instead. Amen.

13 FEBRUARY

Inferiority Complex?

Numbers 13 v 33: We saw the Nephilim there… We seemed like grasshoppers in our own eyes, and we looked the same to them.

When Moses sent out the twelve leaders to explore the 'promised land', on their return, even though they spoke of all the good things the land produced, ten of the men chose to focus on the negative aspect. They were going to have to deal with some rather large and strong inhabitants – the Nephilim!

These men were looking at their own strength and ability to overcome the giants and said they couldn't do it, as they were far too small and weak to stand up against the Nephilim. However, these ten leaders were mistaken, for they were not looking to God and what He could do.

Do you ever feel inferior to others and think that you can't do anything for the Lord? Do you feel inadequate in any way? This is not how God sees you and not how he wants you to see yourself. For in and through Him you can do all things!

Please forgive me Lord, for looking at myself in such a negative way, instead of seeing who I am in You. Amen.

14 FEBRUARY

With God on Our Side

Numbers 14 v 9: Only do not rebel against the LORD. And do not be afraid of the people of the land, because we will swallow them up. Their protection is gone, but the LORD is with us. Do not be afraid of them.

Joshua and Caleb not only saw the goodness of the promised land, they saw God's hand delivering them from the Nephilim that were living there, and so were pleading with the people to trust in God and not to be afraid, for they can surely take the land.

Sadly the people refused to listen and remained in fear. As a result of this, not one of them entered the 'promised land' except for Joshua and Caleb – forty years later. Their lack of faith cost them a lot!

Is there something you are afraid of doing for God, even though he has said you can do it? Then learn from the Israelites' mistake and step out in faith, for God is on your side and you can do it.

Dear Lord, when things look too much for me, may I immediately turn to You, trusting that you will help me, despite my fear. Thank you so much for showing me that I need not be afraid. Amen.

15 FEBRUARY

God's Heartache

Numbers 14 v 11: The LORD said to Moses, "How long will these people treat me with contempt? How long will they refuse to believe in me, in spite of all the miraculous signs I have performed among them?"

It does seem incredible, doesn't it, that the Israelites had seen God come through for them time after time and in the most amazing ways, and yet they still didn't trust him or believe that he could help them against these giants!

Are there any situations in your life now that you don't believe God can change, or do anything about?

We can see just how much it hurts our Lord when we fail to believe he can come through for us, so why do we do it? He longs for us to trust in Him, just as a small child trusts in their parent.

If you are struggling in this area, then please join with me in this prayer today.

O Heavenly Father, please forgive me for the hurt I have caused you through my doubt and unbelief. I want to Trust in you more and more each day; please help me. Amen.

16 FEBRUARY

Rebellion in the Camp

Numbers 16 v 3: They came as a group to oppose Moses and Aaron and said to them, "You have gone too far! The whole community is holy, every one of them, and the LORD is with them. Why then do you set yourselves above the LORD's assembly?"

What causes rebellion against leaders? It usually stems from pride and jealousy; from wanting the position of power, thinking you can do a much better job than they are doing. Have you ever sensed any of these feelings arising within? I think, if we're totally honest, we all have from time to time.

Whenever we rebel against those in spiritual authority over us, we are in fact rebelling against God; for they hold their position by His divine appointment.

This group of rebels thought they had it all worked out, but they were self-deceived and in effect, digging their own graves!

O Lord, please purge from me any seeds of pride, jealousy or outright rebellion. May you give me a reverential fear of those in authority over me and may I gladly submit to their authority, for your name's sake. Amen.

17 FEBRUARY

Look Up!

Numbers 21 v 9: So Moses made a bronze snake and put it up on a pole. Then when anyone was bitten by a snake and looked at the bronze snake, he lived.

It was because the Israelites had grumbled against God and Moses that they were now being bitten by these snakes. They had cried out to Moses and he had prayed for them and God had shown him to make a bronze snake and put it on a pole. So now if an Israelite was bitten, instead of facing death he could look at the snake and live!

God had made a way for them to be saved. If they wasted their time looking at the snake bite and worrying about how bad it was and how big it was getting, then it would be too late for them to be saved but if they looked away from their problem and straight up at the snake they would survive!

Next time you have a problem, look up to Jesus and let Him help you!

O Lord, this is such a picture of what Jesus has done for us on the cross. Thank you Lord for providing me with this chance of life. Amen.

18 FEBRUARY

Surprised by God!

Numbers 22 v 28: Then the LORD opened the donkey's mouth, and she said to Balaam, "What have I done to you to make you beat me these three times?"

Just when you thought God couldn't surprise you any more - you read that he enabled a donkey to speak! How amazing is that! And yet, in a way, should we be surprised? After all, God is God and he can do whatever he wants, and he can use anyone or anything he chooses!

If you have been telling yourself that God couldn't possibly use you and that you are no good at anything – then think of the donkey and how God used her that day! He will surprise you too, in the way he uses you!

We need to be ready and alert to whatever God is doing in our lives – open to new ways of hearing from Him and open to new ways of being used by Him. For nothing is impossible with God – only believe!

Forgive me Father if I have kept you in a neat little box and not expected to be surprised by you. Forgive me too, if I've felt you couldn't use me. If you can use a donkey, you can certainly use me! Amen.

19 FEBRUARY

Someone You Can Trust

Numbers 23 v 19: God is not a man, that he should lie, nor a son of man, that he should change his mind. Does he speak and then not act? Does he promise and not fulfil?

It is a horrible thing to be let down, lied to and betrayed by someone we really thought we could trust. Someone who loved us and, we thought, had our best interests at heart. If an enemy hurts us we can endure it, but when it's someone very close to you, the wounds go very deep.

The truth is, people will always let us down on some level or other – for no one is perfect. But God will never let us down, as our verse for today tells us. He won't change his mind; with Him a promise is a promise and he will never lie to us. How comforting for us to know, that there is someone who always has our best interests at heart, someone who will always be there for us – someone who we can fully Trust!

Thank you Father, that when those I love let me down, I can always turn to You, knowing that you will never let me down. Amen.

20 FEBRUARY

Everything Must Go!

Numbers 33 v 55: But if you do not drive out the inhabitants of the land, those you allow to remain will become barbs in your eyes and thorns in your sides. They will give you trouble in the land where you will live.

God knew that the Israelites would suffer in the land if they did not deal with their enemies. Just one enemy in the camp, would be one too many!

We have lots of enemies in our lives; several are within us. Enemies such as jealousy, un-forgiveness, pride and self-pity, to name but a few. Or there may be people in our lives that God has told us to no longer have a relationship with, as they are draining the life out of us or are a bad influence on us.

It would be a good time now to ask God what things or people he would like to drive out from your life.

Thank you Lord for opening my eyes to this today. I come before you now and ask you to show me anything, or anyone, I have allowed to remain in my life that should not be there and give me the strength of character to deal with it, in Jesus' name. Amen.

21 FEBRUARY

God's Boundaries

Numbers 34 v 2: Command the Israelites and say to them: "When you enter Canaan, the land that will be allotted to you as an inheritance will have these boundaries…"

God places boundaries around our lives and, if viewed correctly, they give us a deep sense of security. It is only when they are breached that we will find ourselves out of our depth and struggling. For our heavenly Father has specific areas he wants us to be in and some he does not; he only wants what is ultimately the best for us.

Are there any places you know the Lord doesn't want you to be, but you are tempted to go there anyway? Maybe it looks more exciting? But God's boundaries are there to protect you, to keep you safe from harm.

I believe God has a special place for each one of us, where we can blossom and flourish and come into all he has prepared for us! Who would not want that?

O Father, forgive me when I think I know what's best for me. I thank you that you know exactly where I should be; may I be secure and content in this place. Amen.

22 FEBRUARY

Time to Move On

Deuteronomy 1 v 6: The LORD our God said to us at Horeb, "You have stayed long enough at this mountain."

There is a time to stay and a time to move on. Quite often we stay far too long in a place when God has finished with us there, and is now asking us to move on!

God knows that we will begin to stagnate if we remain in one place for too long – we need a 'new' place with fresh experiences and different people to meet, where he can teach us new things about Himself. Staying in the same place beyond God's allotted time for us will result in our lives being dry and unproductive.

God has made us for 'change', and it could well be today that God is saying to you "It's time to move on!"

O Lord, please show me when I've been in a place, situation or relationship for too long. Please show me very clearly when it is time to move on. I don't want to miss out on your plans for my life by being stubborn and refusing to move. May I be both willing and open to receiving your guidance for my life. Amen.

23 FEBRUARY
Nothing Added, Nothing Taken Away

Deuteronomy 4 v 2: Do not add to what I command you and do not subtract from it, but keep the commands of the LORD your God that I give you.

God's Word is so very precious, that we should guard it in its entirety. There are grave dangers if we try to add extra commands – this was something the Pharisees were guilty of. Similarly, nothing from His word should ever be removed, simply because it doesn't happen to meet with our approval. As Timothy warned us – many will give up sound doctrine and gather teachers around them who will teach only what they desire to hear!

We also need to be aware of these twin dangers when we are seeking personal guidance from the Lord. When he gives us a scripture we may be tempted to read on further until we get the answer we want, or we may be tempted to only take the parts we like from it. Don't do it!

Thank you for your commands Lord – for all of them! May I love your Word so much that I will never entertain the idea of either adding or taking away from it, and please show me if I am ever in danger of doing this. Amen.

24 FEBRUARY

Close to You

Deuteronomy 4 v 7: What other nation is so great as to have their gods near them the way the LORD our God is near us whenever we pray to him?

The Lord chose the Israelites to be His own special people, not because of anything that they had done, but to demonstrate to the world that he wanted to have a relationship with us.

'Religion' will try and find ways to reach God, whereas God is actually right here waiting for us – He is only a prayer away! How amazing is that? The God who created the whole universe wants to be in a close relationship with me! And he wants to be that close to you too!

Is this closeness something you experience or is it still something you dream of? Well today you can be as close to God as you want to be - He is waiting just for you! As you draw near to Him, He will draw near to you.

O Lord God, I thank you that you are My God and that you want to be close to me; it seems too wonderful to be true, but it is! May I be more willing to draw close to you and in doing so be aware of your closeness to me. Amen.

25 FEBRUARY

True Love

Deuteronomy 6 v 5: Love the LORD your God with all your heart and with all your soul and with all your strength.

What is love? What is true love? Is it a warm fuzzy feeling or a feeling of great passion? Today's verse gives us an insight into how God views love and tells us how he desires us to love Him!

Our love for God should be all consuming. He wants us to love Him with every fibre of our being – holding nothing back! He isn't satisfied with us loving him just a little – he wants us to love him with our whole heart.

Do you have a burning passion for God? If we are totally honest, most of us probably don't, but I wonder how our lives would be changed if we took God's word seriously and started to love God with all we possess? What transformation would it bring into our lives and the lives of those around us?

Dear Father, your word has stirred something within me today – I see how far my love for you falls short. Please forgive me Lord and ignite a fire of love for you deep down in my heart. Amen.

26 FEBRUARY

Foolish Pride

Deuteronomy 8 v 17-18: You may say to yourself, "My power and the strength of my hands have produced this wealth for me." But remember the LORD your God, for it is he who gives you the ability to produce wealth...

Oh how our pride deceives us; it makes us falsely believe that 'It's all about me and what I have achieved!' How slyly it creeps up on us and takes us captive to its thoughts! It's such a gradual process that we barely perceive it has occurred.

We may begin earnestly seeking our God and fully relying on Him for everything, but as we gain confidence and become successful, we slowly start to rely on our own strength and become confident in ourselves rather than God. We forget that it is God who has given us success. For without God we can do nothing.

I confess, I do see this pattern at work in my life – thank you Lord for revealing this to me today. Please forgive me for indulging in it, may your Holy Spirit convict me as soon as any form of pride begins to emerge, so I can nip it in the bud immediately. Amen.

27 FEBRUARY

Love Always Protects

Deuteronomy 23 v 5: However, the LORD your God would not listen to Balaam but turned the curse into a blessing for you, because the LORD your God loves you.

This verse is so reassuring and comforting – it lets us know how protected and secure we are in God's love. He will not allow anything that comes against us to ultimately succeed.

For any negative situation you may be in right now, God can turn it round and bring more blessings from it than you could possibly imagine!

Why does God do this? It's not as if we deserve it. We are told it's because He loves us! Let's take a moment to really let that soak in. He loves us!

Thank you Lord for the amazing sense of 'peace' and 'comfort' this brings me - knowing that you have everything that affects me in your hands and that anything that rises up against me, You will put down. Thank you that Your love always protects. Amen.

28 FEBRUARY

Don't Get Side Tracked

Deuteronomy 28 v 14: Do not turn aside from any of the commands I give you today, to the right or to the left, following other gods and serving them.

When Satan sees us resolutely following after God in obedience, he is not at all happy and he will do his utmost to take us off in another direction.

Have you ever sensed this happening in your own walk with God? He asks you to do something specifically for Him and suddenly you find yourself being pulled in many different directions. They will usually be 'good' things you're being led away to do – which cleverly makes you think that it must be alright to do them. Be very aware of this tactic of the enemy – for he is very crafty and an expert in the art of deception!

We need to stay close to God and finish what he's given us to do, without being diverted from our course.

It's so easy Lord to become distracted and led in the wrong direction without realising what's really going on. Please help me recognise when I'm being led astray and keep me on the straight path – following after you. Amen.

29 FEBRUARY

Remember!

Deuteronomy 29 v 5: During the forty years that I led you through the desert, your clothes did not wear out, nor did the sandals on your feet.

Why do we so often worry? Why do doubts creep into our minds? – "Will God really come through for me this time?" – "Can I fully trust him?" If we stop and remember the many things the Lord has already done for us – the miracles he has performed during our lives – the worry and doubt will soon flee.

When the Israelites were in the desert for those forty years they had no one else but God – they were totally reliant on Him for all their needs. As we read in today's verse – even their clothing and footwear didn't wear out in all that time!

Try and make it a practice to look back over your own walk with God, maybe even jotting down the things he has done for you and the way he has intervened in those impossible situations you have encountered along the way.

Thank you Lord for reminding me today, of just how faithful you have been. Whenever worries or doubts start to rise within me, please help me remember that you have always come through for me - supplying all my needs. Amen.

01 MARCH

Let God Be God

Deuteronomy 29 v 29: The secret things belong to the LORD our God, but the things revealed belong to us and to our children for ever, that we may follow all the words of this law.

We very much want to know everything these days, but we need to accept that there are some things that only God knows – things we are not meant to know, things we wouldn't be able to understand or take in. We need to accept this fact and let God be God and humbly recognise our human limitations.

God has revealed so much to us, and continues to reveal things so that we will never run out of new revelations from him until we leave this world.

Stop wanting to know everything and trust God with the things unknown; anything he wants us to know he will tell us! Let us instead, rejoice in what we do know!

Heavenly Father, I turn away now from trying to figure everything out and wanting to know all the answers. Instead, I choose today to trust you with everything I don't understand and You will show me whatever I need to know. Thank you Lord. Amen.

02 MARCH

You Can Do It

Deuteronomy 30 v 11: Now what I am commanding you today is not too difficult for you or beyond your reach.

Everyone needs encouraging, especially when the road ahead looks unsure and there's a difficult task to accomplish or you are stepping out into something new. Isn't it good to know that our Lord will never give us something to do that he won't enable us to achieve? With that knowledge alone, all doubt and apprehension should flee!

Have you come up against a wall? Do you feel you can't go on? - that it's all too much? Well it's time to call on God's resources for he will equip you with all you need for the task in hand. He will help you, but you need to ask him.

O Lord it is so comforting to know that you are there for me, encouraging me along the way, giving me all I need to complete all you've given me to do. Thank you so much for showing me this today! Amen.

03 MARCH

Constant Companion

Deuteronomy 31 v 8: The LORD himself goes before you and will be with you; he will never leave you nor forsake you. Do not be afraid; do not be discouraged.

I wonder, when considering the presence of God in our lives, do we rely on our feelings too much? Do we 'sense' God is distant or 'feel' he is no longer there for us? God's Word clearly states that he will never leave us nor forsake us and we either take God at His Word or we don't!

Our God is not only with us all the time but he also goes before us, so we need not fear as we step forward into the unknown – oh what a comfort this is! If we could really grasp the full wonder of this truth – what an immediate sense of 'peace' we would know! We truly would never need to fear again, because we would know for certain that God has everything covered.

There is no one like you God, who is always there for me in each and every situation. I can't begin to thank you enough, for it goes beyond words - the value of this truth! May I let today's verse soak deep within me, that I may draw on it whenever I'm tempted to doubt. Amen.

04 MARCH

Our Rock

Deuteronomy 32 v 4: He is the Rock, his works are perfect, and all his ways are just. A faithful God who does no wrong, upright and just is he.

In a world where there is so much uncertainty and instability how we need to have some sense of security! But true security will never be found in anything this world has to offer. The banks will let you down, the governments will let you down, employers will let you down, our homes may be taken from us and even our own families may let us down. Only God can provide us with real security!

God will always do what is right – he will remain faithful to us and treat us justly. So why is it we so quickly turn to this world for our security? Why not fully trust in God, who we know will never fail us?

If ever there's a time to know God as our Rock, it is now! So I am asking you today – to recognise where your true sense of security lies – in God alone!

I confess Lord I have placed my security in the things of this world far too much, help me change this so that all my security is in you – my Rock. Amen.

05 MARCH

Backslidden?

Deuteronomy 32 v 6: Is this the way you repay the LORD, O foolish and unwise people? Is he not your Father, your Creator, who made you and formed you?

When all was going well for Israel they began to forget what God had done for them; they began to follow the ways of the peoples around them. This can happen to us too, and it usually does so very gradually and insidiously, so we barely notice how far back we have fallen.

How near to God are you today? Are you aware of him as your Father and Creator? Or has God become somewhat distant and remote to you? Or maybe you are somewhere in between? Wherever you find yourself today, know that God loves you and all he wants is for you to love him back. Yes, it's that simple!

If you recognise that you have backslidden, come back to God today and tell him how sorry you are and he will welcome you home!

O Father, I never want to leave your side again. Please make me aware as soon as I start to drift away from you; I just want to love you and be loved by you. Please hold me close. Amen.

06 MARCH

Wherever You Go

Joshua 1 v 9: Have I not commanded you? Be strong and courageous. Do not be terrified; do not be discouraged, for the LORD your God will be with you wherever you go.

When in familiar places it is easier to believe that God is with you and you can often associate these places with his presence. However, when we find ourselves in new territory with challenging situations, experiencing things we never have before, it can be quite a different story – it may well seem as though God has abandoned us. But this is totally untrue for, as the scripture tells us today, God is with us wherever we go!

Are you perhaps in a new and frightening place right now? Are you struggling to find God in your current situation? Then take heart – for he IS with you and with Him by your side you have no need to fear. He has everything in His hands!

Thank you so much Father for the promises in your word. May I be encouraged today in knowing I have you with me wherever I may go. However strange or dark it may be, you are still there right by my side. Amen.

07 MARCH

Memory Stones

Joshua 4 v 24: He did this so that all the peoples of the earth might know that the hand of the LORD is powerful and so that you might always fear the LORD your God.

To help the people of Israel remember what God had done to enable them to cross the Jordan, twelve stones were taken from the dried up river and set up at Gilgal.

Joshua told the people that the stones were to be a reminder for future generations and indeed for all the peoples of the earth, of God's mighty power. As a result they would be filled with a reverential fear of their God.

Can you recall times in your own life when God has acted on your behalf in a most powerful way? Maybe you could think up some ways to remember these events for your own encouragement, and also for future generations?

May I never take for granted the amazing things you've done in my life Lord, and may I never lose my sense of awe of You. Please help me to remember and to pass on the good news to the next generation. For your glory! Amen.

08 MARCH

He Has You Covered

Joshua 5 v 12: The manna stopped the day after they ate this food from the land; there was no longer any manna for the Israelites, but that year they ate of the produce of Canaan.

The Lord knows just what we need, when we need it and for how long we need it! How good it is to know that God has us covered!

As soon as the Israelites reached the 'promised land' and were able to eat of its produce, they no longer needed the heaven-sent manna and from that moment on the manna ceased to fall.

Do we sometimes take for granted how well we are taken care of by our heavenly Father? Whatever your needs are today, know that the Lord will provide for you at just the right time, and just what you need. It won't arrive a moment too soon or a moment too late, for he knows how best to look after you; better than you do yourself!

Thank you Lord, for how you have kept me and fed me with just what I need; not only physically but also spiritually. You are an amazing God! Amen.

09 MARCH

Sin in the Camp!

Joshua 7 v 13: ... That which is devoted is among you, O Israel. You cannot stand against your enemies until you remove it.

Although Achan's sin was carried out in secret and he had hidden away the things he had taken, God knew and ended up exposing his sin very publicly! Because of this one man's sin, the whole of Israel was affected and suffered as a result, for they were routed by their enemies.

God knows about our secret sins too and although you may not think so, they will affect other people! Also, whatever is hidden now, God will eventually bring out into the open; so maybe today is a good opportunity to deal with any hidden sin in your life.

If you sense the Lord prodding you at all today, then please don't let this pass by. If you need to share things with a trusted friend, then speak with them and ask them to pray with you. It's not too late to put things right.

O Father, we all sin and need to keep short accounts with you.
Please reveal to me any sin that is hidden within me this day,
that I may deal with it, by turning completely away from it, in
Jesus' name. Amen.

10 MARCH

Looks Can Be Deceptive!

Joshua 9 v 14: The men of Israel sampled their provisions but did not enquire of the LORD.

This story has so much to teach us today, that I thoroughly recommend reading the whole of the chapter. It shows us just how clever our enemy is - how easily we can be deceived and that we shouldn't always trust what is presented to us, however convincing it may appear. It also teaches us how dangerous it is to leave God out of the equation when making major decisions.

Because the Israelites didn't enquire of the Lord, but instead relied on their own insight, they had to continually live alongside their enemies. Don't always accept things at face value, for no one is exempt from being deceived and we need to stop and ask God before we rush into things, or we too may be faced with the negative consequences!

If you have a major decision to make, then please take the time to step back a little and ask God what he wants you to do. Don't make the same mistake as the Israelites!

Thank you Lord for this powerful story from Israel's history. May I take it to heart and learn the lessons from it in my own life. Amen.

11 MARCH

Why Are You Waiting?

Joshua 18 v 3: So Joshua said to the Israelites: "How long will you wait before you begin to take possession of the land that the LORD, the God of your fathers, has given you?"

There were still seven tribes of Israel that had yet to receive their inheritance and Joshua asks them, in effect, 'what are you waiting for?' The land was already theirs for the taking, so what was stopping them?

I wonder what is stopping you from moving out into all that God has for you; is there something he has placed in your heart to do? Are there promises he's made to you, and yet you have still not stepped out into them?

I strongly believe God is speaking to many of you today, and he would say to you – 'Now is the time to step out and take the land I have given you. Don't hold back any longer, for I have placed it all there for you to walk in and claim as your own - it is your inheritance in Me!'

Dear Father, forgive me for allowing things to hold me back from entering into all that you have for me. I come against any fear or self-doubt and I choose to step out in faith, knowing you are with me. Amen.

12 MARCH

Promise Keeper

Joshua 21 v 45: Not one of all the LORD's good promises to the house of Israel failed; every one was fulfilled.

There are not many people or establishments you can fully trust these days. People often won't keep their promise to you, neither will politicians or governments – the list goes on and on. But there is one person who will never let you down; one person who will keep all their promises and that is the Lord our God. Aren't you glad there are no promises God won't keep? For our God is faithful and just and will keep every promise he has made to you, just as he did to his chosen people – Israel!

This is of great comfort to us and we will be truly blessed if we meditate on today's verse, for it will greatly increase our faith and our sense of security in God.

Maybe you are reading this today and find yourself still waiting for God to fulfil his promise to you? Take heart from this verse, for it will come to pass - just as he said!

How comforting to know you won't fail me Lord; that you won't break any of your promises to me; that your promises will all be fulfilled. Thank you Lord! Amen.

13 MARCH

Yield Your Heart

Joshua 24 v 23: "Now then," said Joshua, "throw away the foreign gods that are among you and yield your hearts to the LORD, the God of Israel."

The Israelites had made a decision, along with Joshua, that they were going to wholeheartedly serve the Lord and not the gods of the nations they had driven out from the land. There was no room for any other gods, for the Lord wanted their 100% commitment, much as a husband wants from his wife! God wants us to be faithful to him and not to be led astray to serve and worship anyone or anything else.

Today would be a good day to stop and take stock of your life. What percentage does God have of your heart? He wants it ALL! It would also be a good day to throw away anything that hinders our walk with the Lord; anything that may be drawing us away from Him. Do you have any such things in your life?

O Father I want to follow you with my whole heart. Please help me to throw away anything that hinders that and show me anything else that also needs to go. Amen.

14 MARCH

It's a Test!

Judges 2 v 22: I will use them to test Israel and see whether they will keep the way of the LORD and walk in it as their forefathers did.

Israel had failed to follow all of the Lord's commands and as a result he didn't allow them to drive out any more of their enemies – but allowed them to stay, so as to 'test' Israel.

I believe the Lord often does a similar thing in our lives. He doesn't remove all of our problems and he leaves people in our lives that we find difficult, to see if we will continue to follow Him and remain faithful to Him. This he does in love in order that our faith might become stronger, so when a really serious trial comes along we will already know how to dig in to God.

Are you frustrated when things are going wrong in your life? Well maybe look at it differently – see it as a chance to grow closer to God and show his glory, through the way you handle these things!

Please help me Father, to see your hand in my problems and realising that you are allowing them in order to test me - to see if my heart still turns towards You. Amen.

15 MARCH

Trust in God Alone

Judges 4 v 8: Barak said to her, "If you go with me, I will go; but if you don't go with me, I won't go."

Barak had been told by God, through Deborah, to go up to Mount Tabor and God would give Israel's enemy into his hands. However, Barak didn't feel confident enough to go without his spiritual leader, Deborah, thereby placing his trust in Deborah rather than directly in God's word to him. The result was Israel's enemy being given into the hands of a woman, and Barak losing the honour he would otherwise have received had he fully trusted in God.

Are we in danger of doing the very same thing? It can be very subtle. Maybe we begin to focus more on what our pastor is saying and doing than on what God is telling us to do? Maybe we come to rely on those in spiritual authority over us rather than on God Himself? No matter how spiritual a person may seem to us, we must make sure we are not placing our faith in them, rather than in God.

Thank you for opening my eyes today to the dangers of worshipping my spiritual leaders. May I trust in you alone Lord, for only You are worthy! Amen.

16 MARCH

In God's Eyes

Judges 6 v 12: When the angel of the LORD appeared to Gideon, he said, "The LORD is with you, mighty warrior."

Gideon certainly didn't see himself as a 'mighty warrior' (see verse 15) - even though that is what his name meant – but God DID!!!

This is so important for us to take in today. God sees our potential and sees what we can become once fully submitted to Him and His will. He created us, so knows us far better than we know ourselves He knows how he's wired us and what makes us tick!

So often we rate ourselves by how we see ourselves – but maybe we need to ask God how He sees us? You may feel weak and the least important – but take heart – you are just the person God wants to use!

Can this really be true Father; that although I feel inadequate and unfit for anything, you really see me as someone who can do mighty things for you? Please help me take this in Lord, and to really believe it. Amen.

17 MARCH

God's Amazing Patience

Judges 6 v 39: Then Gideon said to God, "Do not be angry with me. Let me make just one more request. Allow me one more test with the fleece."

Gideon had been told by God that he would save the Israelites by his hand, but Gideon wanted to be totally sure he'd heard God correctly, so he asked God to confirm his word to him by 'putting out a fleece' not once but twice!

The first time he asked for the fleece to become wet with dew, while the ground would remain dry and God did this. Then the second time he asked God to make the ground wet and keep the fleece dry and God did this also!

The Lord showed amazing patience towards Gideon and his doubtful mind. Obviously God would prefer us to accept his word at face value, but he understands those who lack confidence and so graciously answers Gideon's requests, not once but twice! What a mighty God we serve!

Thank you Lord, for your amazing patience with me. Whenever I doubt that I've heard from you and keep asking for confirmations, I know you understand me. Amen.

18 MARCH

Don't Put God in a Box

Judges 14 v 4: His parents did not know that this was from the LORD...

Samson desired a wife from among the Philistines, Israel's enemy, and his parents were understandably upset about this, strongly believing it to be wrong for their son. But, they had not realised that this was all part of God's plan!

There is a great lesson for us here, as it can be very easy to assume we know what God wants us to do with our lives and also what he doesn't want, but we may be wrong! He may ask us to do something that, on the face of it, seems to go completely against the grain, but we must never put God in a box, of our own thoughts and ideas. His ways are far above our ways and his thoughts above our thoughts. Who are we to tell God he's got it wrong?

What we really need to do is discern His voice over and above any other voices that may be clamouring for our attention.

O Lord, I had never really thought about this before, that you might want to work outside the box! May I always remember that you are God and can do whatever you please. Help me to hear your voice more clearly. Amen.

19 MARCH

There's Always Hope

Judges 16 v 22: But the hair on his head began to grow again after it had been shaved.

Everything had worked out badly for Samson! After finally giving in to Delilah's constant nagging, the Philistines had come upon him and cut off his hair so that his strength was all gone - meaning God was no longer with him. The Philistines then gouged out his eyes and led him away captive. Not much to hope for now!

But the hair on Samson's head began to grow again and, as a result, his strength returned and he was able to conquer his enemy at last! Even though it cost him his own life, he had saved Israel from the hands of the Philistines.

What can we learn from this story? If we have messed up and let God down, it doesn't mean he's finished with us. We mustn't give up hope, because he can still use us for His glory, it's not too late! Your 'hair' can grow back!

Thank you for the encouragement this story affords Lord. Help me to never give up hope, however desperate a situation may appear. Help me to see what you are going to bring about through it. Amen.

20 MARCH

Good Choice

Ruth 1 v 14: At this they wept again. Then Orpah kissed her mother-in-law goodbye, but Ruth clung to her.

After the tragic loss of their husbands, Naomi had urged both her daughters-in-law to return to their own mothers' homes, but they responded very differently! Orpah returned, but Ruth refused to leave and clung to her mother-in-law! She was willing to leave her own family and homeland and go to a strange land; she even told Naomi that her God would become her God! As a result of Ruth's kindness, she became married to a kind, loving and good man. She had put someone else's needs before her own and in return God had richly rewarded her!

I wonder, are you facing a similar decision in your life right now? Wondering which path to take? If we give ourselves to others and their needs, God will reward us beyond all measure. We often have to make difficult choices that will affect the lives of those around us. May we put others first and look to their needs before our own, for if we do, we will surely be blessed!

O Heavenly Father, please help me to make good choices - to put others' needs before my own, even when this hurts. O how I need you Lord. Amen.

21 MARCH

Prayer Changes Everything

1 Samuel 1 v 18: ... Then she went her way and ate something, and her face was no longer downcast.

Hannah was desperate for a son; so desperate that she couldn't even eat. She had cried out to the Lord, from the depths of her heart, and promised to give the boy to the Lord for his entire life, if he gave her a son. Eli the priest blessed her as she left the temple and from that moment on Hannah was different! Now she ate again and was no longer downcast; in other words she believed her prayer was going to be answered!

How amazing that Hannah could immediately eat again, the depression had lifted and now she had hope! And all this before there was any evidence of her prayer being answered!

So what does this teach us today? Once we have cried out to the Lord in our desperation, we need to let go, leave the answer in His hands and then receive His peace, which comes from fully trusting he will answer!

O Lord, help me to be like Hannah –so that once I've prayed to you in earnest, I will trust you with the answer and receive your peace. Amen.

22 MARCH

Are You Listening?

1 Samuel 3 v 10-11: ... Then Samuel said, "Speak, for your servant is listening." And the LORD said to Samuel...

How can we hear from God if we are not listening? How do we really hear what others are saying to us? Firstly we need to be still, and then empty all our own thoughts, ideas and feelings, before we can truly begin to hear what is being said by the other person. It is exactly the same when it comes to hearing from God!

So many of us long to hear God's voice; but are we willing to stop, be still, and listen? Our lives are generally so busy and full of noise that it makes listening very difficult; which is why we need to set aside some quiet space in our day where we can be alone with the Lord. We can then sit in His presence and say, like Samuel, "Speak for your servant is listening." Then we will hear that still small voice speaking words into our mind, words we don't recognise as our own – for they will be His!

O how I long to hear your voice speaking to me personally Lord. Please help me to set aside some time that I can spend just with you, where I can empty myself of my own concerns and come and listen to what's in Your heart. Thank you that you want to talk to me. Amen.

23 MARCH

We Want a King!

1 Samuel 8 v 20: Then we shall be like all the other nations, with a king to lead us and to go out before us and fight our battles.

Israel had never had a king – God had always led them and spoken directly to them through various leaders, prophets and judges; but now Israel wanted to be just like everyone else and have their very own King! They were in essence saying, 'We don't think you're good enough for us God; we want to be just like everyone else around about us.'

Do you find yourself doing the same thing? Wanting to be like others around you; so that you won't be different and stand out from the crowd? Is it easier for you to put your confidence in the ways of this world rather than in God's ways? This was never God's plan for your life. Just as God had chosen Israel to be his own 'unique' people, so he has chosen you to be set apart for Him. He wants you to be different and to stand out; he wants you to fully trust in Him, and not in this world around us.

O Lord, you are my God, and only 'you' can lead me in the right ways. Please forgive me for looking to the ways of this world, instead of to you, for answers. Amen.

24 MARCH

You've Hidden Long Enough!

1 Samuel 10 v 22: ... And the LORD said, "Yes, he has hidden himself among the baggage."

When Samuel came to call out Saul as the very first king of Israel, amazingly he couldn't be found because he was hiding among the baggage!

There are two things to learn from this. One is about us not shrinking back from what God is calling us to do, but being willing to step out under the spotlight. We may feel more comfortable hidden away out of sight, but if God is calling us into a more public form of ministry – we must obey Him!

Secondly, notice how Saul was hidden among the baggage! How often do we get caught up in the baggage of life? There are many things to distract us and draw us away from whatever God is calling us to do. Is God calling you out of the shadows today?

Dear Lord, thank you for challenging me today. May I be fully available to you and be willing to lay aside anything you ask me to, in order that I might follow what you are calling me to do; in Jesus' name. Amen.

25 MARCH

Prayer Matters!

1 Samuel 12 v 23: As for me, far be it from me that I should sin against the LORD by failing to pray for you. And I will teach you the way that is good and right.

Our verse for today gives us a real 'wake up' call and rather shocks us into the realisation of just how important prayer really is! And look how important it is in God's eyes; so important in fact that Samuel calls it a 'sin' not to do it!

We need to bring everything and everyone to God in prayer, for who knows what God may do when we pray? Some people that we know may have no one else praying for them!

If you struggle with prayer, and most of us do, then ask God to help you and give you the desire to pray and to show you who he especially wants you to pray for; He will bring them into your thoughts. This will immediately make your prayer life more exciting! You may even like to keep a prayer journal, so that you can record the results!

Thank you Father, I know you want my prayers to bless others; please give me a new desire to pray. Amen.

26 MARCH

The Fear of Man

1 Samuel 15 v 24: … I was afraid of the people and so I gave in to them.

What a painful lesson Saul learns here. Because he has given in to the people, rather than obeying what God told him to do, he loses the kingdom; that's a big price to pay!

I wonder, are we in danger of letting the 'fear of man' control our lives too? It can be very subtle – we may not even realise we are doing it. Have you ever felt so guilty for not doing what someone has asked that, just to get rid of that awful feeling, you have gone along with it, even though you have clearly felt God didn't want you to? Such is the 'fear of man'! If you recognise this pattern in your own life, then 'today' you can change! Confess your tendency to wanting to please 'man' rather than God and ask God to forgive you. For the 'fear of man' is a snare – it will prevent you from being all that God intended you to be, just as it prevented Saul from continuing to be king! Be delivered from it right now; don't spend one more day under its spell!

O Father God, please hear my prayer and release me today from this 'fear of man' – set me FREE, so that I'm completely free to love and serve you wholeheartedly. Amen.

27 MARCH

The 'Heart' of the Matter

1 Samuel 16 v 7: … Man looks at the outward appearance, but the LORD looks at the heart.

What a great comfort this verse is to all of us who don't rate our outward appearance too highly!

Samuel mistakenly thought the Lord had chosen the best looking of Jesse's sons to be the next king. But no; the Lord had chosen the son not even considered worthy to bring in from the fields where he was tending the sheep, to be shown to Samuel. The Lord chose the one the world would have rejected.

It can be easy to be swayed by appearances, just as Samuel was, but they can often act as a mask, hiding what's really underneath. God wanted a king with a 'heart after his own.' Enter – David!

We must be very careful not to pre-judge someone based on their appearance, because if the Lord looks at the heart then how much more should we!

Thank you Lord for reminding me not to judge by mere outward appearances, but be like you and look beyond, to what's in a person's heart. Amen.

28 MARCH

Be the Real You

1 Samuel 17 v 39: … "I cannot go in these," he said to Saul, "because I am not used to them." So he took them off.

David could not face Goliath wearing Saul's armour, as it wasn't his and he wasn't used to wearing it. What works for someone else doesn't necessarily work for you. Beware of following other peoples' methods; you need to discover God's method for you!

We are individuals, with an individual God-given purpose and we should rejoice in this. We must not let other people pressurize us into following their agenda, even if they mean well. We must be free to move as God intends us to; it's the only way we can fulfil His purpose in our lives!

Is there something you're involved in right now that feels very uncomfortable to you? It just doesn't fit? It doesn't allow you to be who you really are? Then the chances are it isn't right for you. Take a step back and ask the Lord what he wants you to do. He won't fail you, I promise!

I am so grateful to you for showing me this today, Father. It has lifted a weight off my shoulders knowing you want me to be me! Amen.

29 MARCH

In God's Name

1 Samuel 17 v 45: ... but I come against you in the name of the LORD Almighty, the God of the armies of Israel, whom you have defied.

As David approached Goliath he didn't rely on his sling and stones (his own efforts) to slay the giant. No, he came against Goliath in the Name of the Lord. What more power could he possibly need?

It is so important that we don't rely on our own strategies or strength when we are trying to defeat the enemy – for if we rely on ourselves then we will fail. Instead, we need to call on God's help and must realise that without God on our side we already stand defeated.

Whenever you have a problem that seems bigger than you, hand it straight over to God and ask Him to come and intervene; for the battle belongs to the Lord!

O Lord, please forgive me for the times I rely on myself and my own resources rather than looking to You and the power of Your Great Name! Thank you for that Name, the Name that is higher than any other. May I use your name, Lord, whenever I come face to face with the enemy and not hold back. Amen.

30 MARCH

It's Good to Talk!

1 Samuel 19 v 18: When David had fled and made his escape, he went to Samuel at Ramah and told him all that Saul had done to him.

There are times when we find ourselves under such spiritual attack, which can take many different forms, that it is right for us to offload onto another person and seek their support and advice. Yes, God is always there for us, but sometimes he'll use people to minister to us. It is very therapeutic to be able to share our troubles and concerns, as long as we don't begin to depend on people rather than God that is! People can help us in practical ways too, as in David's case. Samuel accompanied him to Naiboth, therefore providing him with protection and support.

May our pride never prevent us from asking for help. We can always ask God who we should turn to, as it may not be wise to share your personal troubles with some people. Choose someone who doesn't gossip about other people and who has Godly wisdom.

Thank you Lord, for giving me people that I can turn to in times of trouble; please give me the courage to do this. Thank you that you often choose to work through others to meet my needs. Amen.

31 MARCH

Share and Share Alike

1 Samuel 30 v 24: ... The share of the man who stayed with the supplies is to be the same as that of him who went down to the battle. All shall share alike.

When David's men went into battle, a third of his men were too exhausted to continue, so they stayed behind. However, when they returned from battle with the plunder, some men said that those who had stayed behind should not receive any of it! But David intervened and said they would share it equally among them and he made this a permanent statute for Israel.

The Lord sees the importance of each one of us, and he understands if some have less stamina than others, for we are all made differently. We all have a part to play, which will be tailor made to suit us and God has many blessings available for all of us, whatever our role. So be encouraged today, God has no favourites and he longs to bless you!

O Father, it is so comforting to know that you understand, more than anyone, how differently we are made. Thank you that you have a heart of compassion for those who are weak and that you defend their cause - may I do likewise. Amen.

01 APRIL

Let God Decide

2 Samuel 2 v 1: In the course of time, David enquired of the LORD. "Shall I go up to one of the towns of Judah?" he asked. The LORD said, "Go up." David asked, "Where shall I go?" "To Hebron," the LORD answered.

As you can see from our verse today, we have a God who communicates with us as much as we communicate with Him! In fact as I wrote those words they spoke to me on another level – we can only hear from God if we take the time to ask Him and then wait and listen for his reply!

Today's verse also shows us that it matters to God, very much, where we live! In fact he is interested in every area of our lives. Have you ever thought of praying about where God wants you to live? And which house he'd like you to live in? This principle applies to any area of your life; our heavenly Father longs for us to involve him in our decision making.

O Lord, this continues to amaze me, that You, the creator of the whole universe, could be interested in such an insignificant thing as where I live – but you are! Father, may I never forget to involve you in all my decisions and please forgive me for the times I haven't. Amen.

02 APRIL

Mighty with the Almighty

2 Samuel 5 v 10: And he became more and more powerful, because the LORD God Almighty was with him.

How often do we look at great men of God and become tempted to think it has something to do with how great 'they' are? Then, do we look at ourselves and think, I could never do anything as amazing as that? Well, we would be wrong on both counts! Because if these 'great' men of God did not have God with them, they would just be mere men, but with God with them they can do great things! Also, if we have the faith that God is with us, then we too can be mighty men of God, just like David.

We can never achieve anything of lasting worth through our own strength and ability, and we need to remember that. However, with God Almighty with us, anything at all is possible. If we give ourselves fully to Him, we will be amazed at what can be achieved!

Thank you Lord for reminding me that I can do anything if you are with me - for You are my strength and my song! May I give myself fully to you Lord and the work you want to do through me, in Jesus' name. Amen.

03 APRIL

Facing Your Battles

2 Samuel 5 v 23: ... so David enquired of the LORD, and he answered, "Do not go straight up, but circle round behind them and attack them in front of the balsam trees."

Before David went up to fight he asked the Lord what he should do, and we would be wise to follow his example.

Maybe you are facing a 'battle' in your life right now and perhaps you already have a plan to launch right into it and sort things out, once and for all? However, it wouldn't do any harm to take a step back for a moment and ask God for His view on the situation. He may not want you to fight this particular battle but just to place it all into his hands; or he may give you a particular strategy for dealing with it, as he did to David in today's verse. Or, he may just say, 'Go ahead!' Whichever answer he gives, it will be the correct one for your current circumstances. So, if you find yourself facing a difficult situation, I would encourage you to seek the Lord and then to follow His advice.

Please forgive me Father for the times I haven't consulted you before dealing with problematic issues in my life. Please help me remember to ask you first. Amen.

04 APRIL

Hold Nothing Back

2 Samuel 6 v 14: David, wearing a linen ephod, danced before the LORD with all his might...

If David ever had any inhibitions, he has certainly lost them now, as he dances before the Lord wearing nothing more than his under garments! He cannot help but give his whole self in praise to his Lord, he holds nothing back. David doesn't care what others think of him, all he cares about is praising God; such is his zeal for the Lord!

Can you recall a time when you felt such a way about God yourself? Or have you always tended to feel rather inhibited when praising God? David isn't just doing a little 'jig' before the Lord, it says he danced with all his might, and David was pretty mighty, so it must've been an amazing sight for the people to see – their king so full of praise and passion for God!

I believe God wants us to abandon ourselves in our praise and worship of him; he longs for us to worship him like this - for us to hold nothing back, but to give Him our all!

I'm sorry Lord that I do tend to become rather inhibited when worshipping you. Please help me to let go and give my very self to you; for this is what you desire – All of me! Amen.

98

05 APRIL

In the Wrong Place

2 Samuel 11 v 1: In the spring, at the time when kings go off to war, David sent Joab out with the king's men and the whole Israelite army. ...But David remained in Jerusalem.

Just this one verse, acts as an important warning to us all. King David should've been at war fighting with his men, but instead he stays at home, and with nothing to do he becomes easy prey for the enemy! With time on his hands David notices a very beautiful woman bathing on a roof and immediately he desires her for himself. This leads him to commit adultery with her, and later to arrange her husband's death.

If we are not following wisdom in any area of our lives then we are unwittingly opening a doorway for Satan; such is the seriousness of disobedience. So, when things start to spiral out of control in our lives it's worth asking ourselves, "Am I where I'm supposed to be?"

Thank you Father, for showing me today, just how important it is to be where I am supposed to be. Please show me if I am acting in rebellion in any area of my life. Amen.

06 APRIL

Any Blind Spots?

2 Samuel 12 v 7: Then Nathan said to David, "You are the man!"

It makes you wonder how David could have been so ignorant of his sin, especially when it involved such obvious things as adultery and murder - but he was! He was totally self-deceived, so deceived in fact, that it took a very powerful story to finally melt his heart and open his eyes to the sins he had committed!

Imagine how you would have felt had you been David. After venting your full fury at this 'heartless' man in the story (see verses 1 - 6), you are then suddenly told – 'You are the man!' It must have felt like a knife going in! However, now that it was out in the open and laid bare before God, David could repent, receive forgiveness and be given a fresh start! And so can you and I - Praise God!

O Heavenly Father, please search my heart and see if there are any hidden sins of which I am unaware. Please send me a 'Nathan' to reveal your truth to me and don't let me continue in ignorance any longer. Please Lord, come and cleanse me by the power of your Holy Spirit. Amen.

07 APRIL

Seek God's Face

2 Samuel 21 v 1: During the reign of David, there was a famine for three successive years; so David sought the face of the LORD.

When bad things happen in our lives there may be many different reasons and we might react in several ways. One of the best things to do when facing distressing circumstances is to take it all straight to God and ask him about it. As we seek His face, he will show us if there is any underlying cause. Sometimes there is no reason; trouble may simply have been allowed to come to test our faith. But it's important to ask the Lord first what the cause may be? It could possibly be due to some hidden sin or maybe neglecting to pray for protection?

In David's case God showed him the famine was a result of Saul putting the Gibeonites to death. Israel had promised to protect the Gibeonites and now through Saul's actions they had broken their promise.

O Lord, this is a sobering thought indeed, that sometimes bad things in my life may be a result of something I have done or, indeed, not done. Help me remember to always seek your face in difficult situations. Amen.

08 APRIL

No Cost; No Sacrifice

2 Samuel 24 v 24: But the king replied to Araunah, "No, I insist on paying you for it, I will not sacrifice to the LORD my God burnt offerings that cost me nothing."

The key word in today's verse is 'cost', for a sacrifice without any cost is no sacrifice at all, which king David makes quite clear to Araunah. David loved God so much that nothing but a proper sacrifice would do; he wanted to give God something that cost him personally!

Perhaps we are tempted in a similar way - to give something that costs us nothing? A true sacrifice is always going to cost us something and if it doesn't then we need to stop calling it as such. I wonder how many of us feel quite pleased with the amount we give to the Lord, but does it hurt? This is very challenging and stops and makes us think – it certainly stops and makes me think!

Thank you Lord, for highlighting the need for my giving to 'cost' me something - whether that may be my time, money, possessions or relationships, or anything else you might choose to ask me to give up for you. Please help me to be willing to give and to keep on giving, because just as David loved you, I love you too Lord! Amen.

09 APRIL

Dressed for Worship

1 Kings 6 v 7: In building the temple, only blocks dressed at the quarry were used, and no hammer, chisel or any other iron tool was heard at the temple site while it was being built.

Just as these blocks were prepared outside and away from the temple before they were used to build the temple – we too need to spend time in preparation before we come into the House of God. In fact, it is necessary to do this so that we can be joined together perfectly with our fellow believers - just as the dressed blocks, when brought into the Holy place, would all be ready to fit neatly together! For like living stones we are all being built into a spiritual house.

Could this possibly be why we find so much friction in the church today? Is it because we haven't taken the time to properly prepare our hearts before entering the house of God? If each of us were properly prepared, I wonder what changes we would see in our churches today?

Thank you for opening my eyes to this today, Lord. May I take it fully to heart and seriously begin to prepare myself before coming into your house. Amen.

10 APRIL

It's His Church!

1 Kings 8 v 11: And the priests could not perform their service because of the cloud, for the glory of the LORD filled his temple.

Have you ever heard people say, "That can't have been of God because it interrupted the sermon."? Well that certainly wasn't the case here! Neither was it the case when Peter was in the middle of preaching to Cornelius and his family, when the Holy Spirit came upon them all.

Who are we to tell God what he can or can't do in His own Church? I wonder, have we become so skilled in managing our services today, that we actually shut God out? Or if he does try to make an appearance, do we put it down to enemy activity because it's interrupting 'our' service? Challenging questions!

O Heavenly Father please forgive us, please forgive me, for the times we have not recognised you in our midst and worse still, thought you were the enemy instead. Take away our preconceived ideas of how church should be; help us to be open to the ministry of Your Holy Spirit and allow You to work amongst us, so we can receive all that You have for us. Amen.

11 APRIL

Guard Your Heart

1 Kings 11 v 4: As Solomon grew old, his wives turned his heart after other gods, and his heart was not fully devoted to the LORD his God...

King Solomon was known for his wisdom, and yet later in his life he somehow allows his wives to manipulate his heart into following their gods; he allows them to draw him away from his own God.

Whether it be your wife, husband or any other person you are in a close relationship with, you need to guard your heart, very closely! Do not become complacent and allow yourself to be led astray by others.

We can so easily find ourselves on a slippery slope away from God before we know it, and other gods may come into our lives without us recognising them for what they are. How sad, that despite Solomon's great start he had such a poor finish. His mistake was marrying women who served and worshipped other gods. May we learn from Solomon's mistake!

Please help me to guard my heart at all times Lord, so that I may not be enticed away from you. Amen.

12 APRIL

God is More Than Able

1 Kings 17 v 4: You will drink from the brook, and I have ordered the ravens to feed you there.

If we ever have any doubts that God will come through for us in our hour of need, when things seem totally impossible, then let us look at today's verse and be encouraged!

Elijah is sent by God into the wilderness during a famine, and although he is near a brook, where will he find food? God tells him that he will order the ravens to feed him there! Elijah needed to fully trust in God, because he had no other means to feed himself - this should so encourage us! Why do we fear that God won't come through for us? He is GOD, and he is able to do anything!!! If he can arrange for ravens to bring food, how much more can he arrange for people to come to our aid.

Thank you Lord, that you are a God who is more than able to meet my every need. Forgive me for the times I haven't trusted you, when I have let fear take over - the fear that you won't provide for me. You are an AMAZING God! Amen.

13 APRIL

Choose Who You Will Follow

1 Kings 18 v 21: … "How long will you waver between two opinions? If the LORD is God, follow him; but if Baal is God, follow him." But the people said nothing.

God does not like double mindedness. He requires us to be fully devoted to him, not to have one foot in his kingdom and the other very much in the world. He wants all of us, not just a part.

I wonder if I am speaking to someone today; you maybe go to church each week and call yourself a Christian, but your life outside of church is no different from any non-Christian? Deep down you know God doesn't have all of you and that you have held on to your own way of doing things without any reference to God. Today he is asking you to choose who you will follow! Please take this opportunity now, and don't be like the people in today's verse who after being challenged by Elijah, said nothing. God wants you to respond!

O Lord, I confess I've had my feet in both camps, but I want to change that today! Please forgive me - I now turn from the ways of this world and I choose to follow you Lord! Amen.

14 APRIL

Don't Give Up!

1 Kings 18 v 44: The seventh time the servant reported, "A cloud as small as a man's hand is rising from the sea."

It hadn't rained for three and a half years when Elijah sent out his servant to look towards the sea, and six times he returned to report seeing nothing! How easy it would've been at this point to give up and to conclude that Elijah had got it all wrong. Maybe you're in that very position today? God's word for you today is Don't Give Up! Don't give up praying for that lost relative; don't give up crying out for that healing; don't give up waiting for God to move in your situation – Keep Going!

Elijah kept on sending his servant out because he trusted in God's word to him that he would send rain. On his seventh trip although the cloud was only small, it meant the rain was coming! So trust in God as you watch and wait for your miracle - even the smallest glimmer of hope is a cause for celebration! Be encouraged today; your breakthrough is on its way!

O Heavenly Father, whenever I begin to lose heart, believing that my prayers aren't being answered, help me to keep going and to persevere; putting my trust in your word to me. Amen.

15 APRIL

Struggling with Depression?

1 Kings 19 v 4: ... He came to a broom tree, sat down under it and prayed that he might die. "I have had enough, LORD," he said. "Take my life; I am no better than my ancestors."

If you have never experienced depression you may struggle to understand it, but it can strike anyone at any time, so it's good to know God's perspective on it.

Elijah is running for his life and is also exhausted; two factors that have led him to feel so defeated. How does God deal with Elijah? Does he tell him to snap out of it and pull himself together? No, the first thing he does is to send an angel to minister to his needs! May I encourage anyone who is feeling depressed today that this is exactly what God wants to do for you too; to help you, not to judge you! Sadly, there can be a lot of misunderstanding in the Church regarding depression. If God didn't judge Elijah, then who are we to judge? God would rather have us be honest and real with him about how we feel, than pretending all's well when it isn't!

What comfort it brings to my soul Lord, to know that you understand how I feel and that you want to take care of my deepest needs; I can't thank you enough. Amen.

16 APRIL

Strengthen Your Position!

1 Kings 20 v 22: Afterwards, the prophet came to the king of Israel and said, "Strengthen your position and see what must be done, because next spring the king of Aram will attack you again."

After we've been through a spiritual battle it is often easy to rest and take things easy for a while, but today's verse is a warning that our enemy has no such plans!

What must we do to strengthen our position in preparation for future attacks? We need to stay close to our God by regularly praying, reading his Word and making sure we have regular fellowship with other believers. As we draw near to God, He will draw near to us and will strengthen us. If we continue to do these things we will remain spiritually alert and fully prepared for any attack that Satan may bring. Sadly, many of us become complacent, and leave ourselves vulnerable and open to defeat.

O Heavenly Father, please forgive me for the times I let you down and let things slide. Impress upon my heart today the importance of spending time with you, in prayer, in reading your word and spending time with other Christians. All of this is for my own good! Amen.

17 APRIL

Boldly Ask!

2 Kings 2 v 9: When they had crossed, Elijah said to Elisha, "Tell me, what can I do for you before I am taken from you?" "Let me inherit a double portion of your spirit," Elisha replied.

Sometimes we are far too reserved; we seem almost frightened to ask God for anything BIG. Not so with Elisha; he didn't hold back for a second. He knew what he wanted and he asked for it – a double portion!!!

I wonder how different our Christian lives would be if we were more like Elisha? Is there something BIG that God has placed on your heart? Something you have a real passion to do for Christ? Are you holding back because it seems too much to ask of God; maybe you don't feel worthy to receive it? Then I dare you Today, to boldly ask for the very thing God is already longing to give you! He wants you to ask him and He will supply all your needs along the way to fulfil the purpose he has for your life.

Dear Father, help me not to hold back, but to boldly ask you Today for the BIG things that I sense you want to do in and through me; in Jesus' name. Amen.

18 APRIL

Salt of the Earth

2 Kings 2 v 20: "Bring me a new bowl," he said, "and put salt in it." So they brought it to him.

There is a problem. The water in the city is bad, it is poisoned – unfit to drink. It needs to be cleansed and healed. The first thing Elisha does is to ask for a new bowl and some salt. Why a new bowl and why salt? He throws the salt into the spring and speaks God's Word over it - proclaiming its permanent healing!

Our world is poisoned by evil; it is not as God intended it to be. He has placed us here, and through Jesus we have been made into new, clean vessels for his use. Now he can fill us with salt and throw us into the world where we can be used to bring healing and cleansing to those around us, as we speak His Word.

You are the salt of the earth! Salt cleanses and purifies; this is how God wants to use you! He wants you to make a difference in His world!

Lord, here I am, fit for purpose, in and through Jesus. Fill me with salt and let me be used to bring healing to your world that so desperately needs it. Thank you, in Jesus' name. Amen.

19 APRIL

Open Our Eyes Lord

2 Kings 6 v 17: And Elisha prayed, "O LORD, open his eyes so that he may see." Then the LORD opened the servant's eyes, and he looked and saw the hills full of horses and chariots of fire all round Elisha.

How many of our fears would simply vanish, if we could see the protection God has placed all around us? Most of them would, I believe, if not all. But because we don't see it, we often feel alone, afraid and vulnerable in times of deep distress or danger.

God wants to open our 'spiritual' eyes today – to see that he does have us under the cover and protection of His wings and that he is there for us always. It is our own perception that leads us to believe the lie – that he isn't.

The truth is - greater are those that are with us, than those that are against us. God has got us covered – we just need to remember this next time we find ourselves up against something bigger than us!

Forgive me Father, when I doubt that you are with me, protecting me and looking out for me. Open my eyes to see this truth each time I find myself in a situation I find overwhelming. Thank you for showing me this today. Amen.

20 APRIL

Good News Is for Sharing

2 Kings 7 v 9: ... We're not doing right. This is a day of good news and we are keeping it to ourselves.

There were four men with leprosy who were facing starvation and so they decided to risk it and venture into the enemy camp to try and find food. To their amazement, when they arrived they saw that the enemy had fled, leaving behind all the food and plunder they could want. They realised they needed to let those back in the city of Samaria know; how could they keep this good news all to themselves when they knew so many were starving?

Does this story stir anything within you? We have the best news possible to share, and yet are we guilty of keeping it to ourselves? Just like the city of Samaria – the World is starving: starving to know about God's love for them, and we have just the food they need! How can we withhold it?

O Lord, please help us to share the Good News with others. Impress on our hearts the urgency of this. People are going to die if they don't know about You and your great love for them. Please lead us to those who are desperate and ready to receive you. May we tell them the Good News – Jesus has died, so that they might live! Amen.

21 APRIL

More Gumption

2 Kings 13 v 19: The man of God was angry with him and said, "You should have struck the ground five or six times; then you would have defeated Aram and completely destroyed it. But now you will defeat it only three times."

Elisha has asked the king to 'strike the ground', but the king stopped after only three strikes; Elisha hadn't told him to stop! If the king had continued, he would have had complete victory over the enemy – instead his victory was limited.

How often, I wonder, do we stop short of all God would have us do? Whether it be in prayer, in helping others or in our ministry? There's a powerful lesson we can learn from this verse today. If we approach things half-heartedly, without putting in any real effort, or we stop before God tells us to – we will be missing out on many opportunities for God to move powerfully in our lives, all because, through the various situations we find ourselves in, we gave up too soon and didn't push through.

Thank you Father, for showing me today that I may be encouraged to press on and not to stop until the work is finished. May Your will be done! Your Victory won! Amen.

22 APRIL

God Can Use You

2 Kings 13 v 21: ... When the body touched Elisha's bones, the man came to life and stood up on his feet.

A corpse is suddenly thrown into Elisha's tomb and the result is amazing - the dead man walks out of the tomb 'Alive' – all because he touched Elisha's bones! If Elisha could be used like this, when he was dead, think how much more God can use you while you are still alive?

With God, Nothing is impossible! If dead bones can have such a miraculous effect – then how about us, whose bones are living? Our bodies are the temple of the Holy Spirit. Think of that - the power of God is within us and we can bring life to those who are spiritually dead as they come into contact with us!

Be encouraged today – God wants to use you and your life matters! You may feel you have nothing to give – but just think of Elisha, dead in his tomb, and how he was still used by God!

O Lord, Nothing is impossible with you and you have made my body a temple of your Holy Spirit. I have all I need to be used by you! May my contact with others bring your blessing into their lives and give them 'true' Life - in you! Amen.

23 APRIL

Under the Carpet

2 Kings 17 v 9: The Israelites secretly did things against the LORD their God that were not right.

Israel 'secretly' sinned against God, it says in today's verse, but with God nothing is really secret, so the Israelites were fooling no one but themselves if they thought they could hide things from God.

We have a phrase, and sometimes actually say 'Let's brush it all under the carpet' – as if that really makes it go away? In reality, it is still there – the dust, dirt and rubbish haven't left the room, they are just under the carpet and will still affect the atmosphere. Just as an asthma sufferer would detect the presence of the dust still in that room – so God detects the presence of sin in our lives, however well we think we may be hiding it. God sees everything; it is impossible to hide anything from Him, so why do we even try? Everything hidden will eventually be brought out into the open; we are only fooling ourselves when we try to hide anything from God.

Please forgive me Lord for ever thinking I could hide anything from you. Today I realise, that my sins lay open before you. I turn away from them all now. Please have mercy on me and forgive me - in Jesus' name. Amen.

24 APRIL

Two-Timing Christians

2 Kings 17 v 41: Even while these people were worshipping the LORD, they were serving their idols.

Have you ever been singing in church and suddenly realised to your horror that your mind has drifted off onto something completely different? I have to confess, I have! I don't think this verse is referring to such a lapse in concentration, but to a much more deep-rooted problem.

Maybe money is your idol, so you don't give your full tithe? Maybe sex is your idol, so while worshipping you are noticing the attractive men or women in a lustful way? Maybe power is your idol, and you are still seething because you haven't been asked to lead a service again? Or maybe worries about your family, friends or work are distracting you from truly worshipping God? God doesn't want us fellowshipping with our problems; he wants us to be faithful to Him and to worship Him Alone!

O Heavenly Father, how subtle the enemy is. We don't even realise how unfaithful we are being towards you, yes, even while supposedly worshipping you! Please forgive us for our two-timing ways Lord. May we worship you in Spirit and in Truth! Amen.

25 APRIL

Don't Ask, Don't Get

1 Chronicles 4 v 10: Jabez cried out to the God of Israel, "Oh, that you would bless me and enlarge my territory! Let your hand be with me, and keep me from harm so that I will be free from pain." And God granted his request.

Wow! This verse can so easily be overlooked, tucked away amongst long lists of names, but what a nugget of gold it is when you find it! Doesn't it just 'glow' at you from the page and encourage you to become much bolder when you pray?

Sometimes I think we do God a great injustice by assuming that he wouldn't answer such a prayer as this on the grounds of it being too self-centred, too selfish even; but we couldn't be more wrong – for God was delighted to answer such a prayer! As the saying goes – 'If you don't ask, you don't get!' After all what's the worst that can happen? God says No! You have nothing to lose and everything to gain – so go ahead and ASK!

Please forgive me Lord, for daring to assume that you wouldn't want to answer a prayer such as Jabez's. Please help me to be bolder in what I ask of you in prayer. Amen.

26 APRIL

Battle Cry!

1 Chronicles 5 v 20: They were helped in fighting them, and God handed the Hagrites and all their allies over to them, because they cried out to him during the battle. He answered their prayers, because they trusted in him.

Why was this battle won? It was won because during the battle they 'cried out' to God. Why did he answer their prayers? Because they 'trusted' him!

We may not find ourselves in a physical battle today, but we regularly face spiritual and emotional ones. Sometimes the fight is very fierce and that's when we need to cry out to God for help, rather than trying to sort it all out in our own strength. We need to trust him and then we will see our deliverance come. Next time you find yourself in such a battle, instead of going straight into panic mode and trying to overcome the problem yourself, try going into prayer mode first and then see the difference it makes! The key word here is 'trust' – trust God to come through for you, and answer your cry!

Thank you Father for this powerful reminder that You are there to help us in our daily struggles in life. Next time I face such a battle, may I cry out to you before I do anything else, and trust that you will answer! Amen.

27 APRIL

Wrong Guide

1 Chronicles 10 v 13-14: Saul died because he was unfaithful to the LORD; he did not keep the word of the LORD, and even consulted a medium for guidance, and did not enquire of the LORD.

Saul was the first King of Israel that God chose, but sadly he did not follow the Lord his God wholeheartedly - he was unfaithful to him. When things started to go wrong for Saul, rather than asking the Lord for help and direction, he instead turned to a 'medium' (someone who contacts dead spirits); this was going directly against God's Word!

There are very strong warnings in God's Word about not consulting mediums, and although it may well be tempting to try and speak to a deceased loved one, or to find out what the future holds for you, if our heavenly Father has told us not to do this then we need to take note – we need to get our help and guidance from Him! Saul's life serves as a stark reminder of this.

O Lord, Saul paid the ultimate price with his life, for disobeying your commands. Thank you that you only want what's best for us. May we remain faithful to you and always turn to You - our ultimate guide! Amen.

28 APRIL

Presents from His Presence

1 Chronicles 13 v 14: The ark of God remained with the family of Obed-Edom in his house for three months, and the LORD blessed his household and everything he had.

The ark of God represented His presence, and just as the household of Obed-Edom was blessed while it remained with them, so too will we be blessed if we welcome God's presence to come and live with us today!

But how do we ensure that we have God's presence with us? By making Him first in our family life and removing anything ungodly from our house that we wouldn't feel comfortable sharing with God. By acknowledging him during our day, thanking him for our meals and praying together as a family. These are just some examples of how we can welcome God into our homes; you can probably think of more - but what a way to be truly blessed!

Thank you for your amazing presence Lord. Please come and fill my home today and show me how I can make you feel even more welcome here, and thank you for longing to bless us as a result. Amen.

29 APRIL

Pride in Numbers?

1 Chronicles 21 v 1: Satan rose up against Israel and incited David to take a census of Israel.

Without realising it, David is incited by Satan to carry out a census; but why was this wrong? Only God could ask for a census to be taken of His people and, as they were counted, they each had to pay a ransom for their life. By inciting David to do this, Satan knew the people of Israel would be punished for not doing so. By tempting the one man he brought about the suffering of many others.

Why was David so tempted? Because numbers appealed to his pride! Are we tempted to take pride in how big our churches are? Are the people in them growing into spiritual maturity? Satan is very clever at distracting us from what really matters. Churches seem to be getting larger and larger – but is this always a sign of God's blessing? Do numbers matter as much as obeying the word of the Lord?

O Father, please protect my heart from taking pride in numbers; it is so easy to do. Please make me aware whenever Satan tries to incite me to disobey your word and distract me from things that really matter. Amen.

30 APRIL

Totally Devoted

1 Chronicles 22 v 19: Now devote your heart and soul to seeking the LORD your God.

Allow me to ask you a personal question today. "How devoted are you to seeking the Lord your God?" Are your heart and soul involved? Maybe you are more than happy to seek God in an intellectual capacity, but you really struggle when it comes to involving your heart and soul - your innermost thoughts and feelings? If your heart and soul are not involved, then you are short-changing yourself, and are missing out on the depth of relationship and even the knowledge that you would otherwise receive from God by seeking him fully.

God wants all of you, and he wants every part of you to seek him; he wants your total devotion to Him.

Will you give it to Him today?

O Lord my God, please help me with this today. You know how I struggle to give you the whole of myself. Help me to give my innermost being to seeking You, that I may have a deeper relationship with you. Amen.

01 MAY

Do the Work!

1 Chronicles 28 v 10: Consider now, for the LORD has chosen you to build a temple as a sanctuary. Be strong and do the work.

Is God asking you to build something for Him? Just as David commanded his son Solomon to build a temple for the Lord, I sense an anointing on this verse today – that God is asking 'you' to build something for him and, as with Solomon, he will show you exactly what to do, if you allow him.

It may not be anything as grand as a temple, but maybe he wants your home to become a sanctuary for him? Or maybe he wants you to start up a special project for him? Whatever it may be, if you sense God is speaking to you today, then please don't let it pass you by – please pursue it and ask God to show you exactly what he wants you to do, and ask someone you trust to pray with you about it.

Thank you Lord for your Word; thank you that it speaks to us today. If you are asking me to get to work on something for you, then please show me and give me everything I need to complete it. Amen.

02 MAY

Details from Above

1 Chronicles 28 v 19: "All this," David said, "I have in writing from the hand of the LORD upon me, and he gave me understanding in all the details of the plan."

Be encouraged today that you can hear from God; that by His Spirit he can make known to you all that you need to know. He can give you detailed plans, just as he did to David for the construction of the temple. God will similarly give you detailed instructions for whatever it is he has asked you to build for him. His Spirit will place in your mind everything you need to know, at the time you need to know it and enable you to write it all down and understand it, all at the same time.

If we are open to the Spirit's promptings, we will find ourselves fully equipped for any task the Lord gives us to do for him - so I encourage you today, to keep listening!

Thank you so much Father, that you not only give me work to do for you, but that you also fully equip me in every detail – for every detail matters. Help me follow your instructions Lord, both carefully and completely. Amen.

03 MAY

What Do You Say?

1 Chronicles 29 v 13: Now, our God, we give you thanks, and praise your glorious name.

How often do you forget to say "Thank you"? It can often happen, especially when you are very busy or stressed. We often encourage young children to do it by reminding them, "What do you say?" because they so easily forget and often need prompting. I wonder if God is sometimes tempted to ask us the same question? For when we stop to think about all he has done for us, we should really be thanking him all the time.

It is important to thank and praise our God, not only for all he has done for us but also for who He is! He is the creator of the universe, the maker of heaven and earth. He is the first and the last, the Almighty God, the All Powerful One! How can I not worship and adore Him?

Thank you, thank you, thank you. I can't thank you enough Lord for all you are, for all you've done and for all that you are going to do. But most of all - thank you for loving me! Amen.

04 MAY

The Power of Repentant Prayer

2 Chronicles 7 v 14: ... if my people, who are called by my name, will humble themselves and pray and seek my face and turn from their wicked ways, then will I hear from heaven and will forgive their sin and will heal their land.

When God moves in great power he very much desires his people to be involved. He has called each one of us to pray and, if we turn from all that distracts us from doing His will and give up those things that we know displease him, then His mighty power will be fully released in our lives - as our 'repentant prayer' comes before him.

I believe he is calling his people today to do just this – to turn from their sin and to earnestly seek Him; to cry out for our nations that they may be healed!

Are you ready?

O Lord, please forgive us our sins and stir up our hearts to pray. Give us your heart for our nations; we call on your dear Name, and may you answer our cry for your glory! Amen.

05 MAY

Fame Leads to Testing

2 Chronicles 9 v 1: When the queen of Sheba heard of Solomon's fame, she came to Jerusalem to test him with hard questions.

When you do well in life not everybody will be happy for you; jealousy will be aroused in some, others will be just waiting for you to fail. So don't be surprised when you face testing times in your life, for if God is blessing you abundantly, this is bound to occur.

Others may resent how gifted you are or find it hard to believe; but remember where your gifts have come from. It was God who gave Solomon his great Wisdom, and God who gifted you too! So, thank Him for the gifts he has given you and He will help you through your times of testing – just as He helped Solomon.

O Heavenly Father, thank you for all the gifts and talents you have given me. May I not be surprised if I face all kinds of tests and trials because of them, and may I know who to turn to for help during them, in Jesus' name. Amen.

06 MAY

Heart Trouble

2 Chronicles 12 v 14: He did evil because he had not set his heart on seeking the LORD.

Although this verse may sound rather negative, it nevertheless holds within it a great deal of Wisdom, for it shows us the root of our problems - how we can so easily be enticed away and induced to sin. It acts as a warning bell.

If, like Rehoboam, we don't have our hearts set towards seeking God, if we are not determined to seek him above all else, to know him and what he's saying to us, then we too will become easy prey and may well be drawn into doing what is evil in God's sight.

It is our hearts that God wants; hearts that are after his very own. When we seek Him, we shall become more like Him.

Why not make it your aim to seek God daily in your life?

O Lord, may my 'heart' seek you daily and may it find you. May I wake each morning wanting to know more of you and your ways and desiring your direction in my life for this day and every day. Amen.

07 MAY

Fully Rely on God

2 Chronicles 14 v 11: ... LORD, there is no-one like you to help the powerless against the mighty. Help us, O LORD our God, for we rely on you...

Are you feeling powerless today? Have things in your life got so out of hand that you are feeling completely overwhelmed by them? Do you feel so under attack that there is nothing more you can do? Well, be encouraged by today's verse taken from King Asa's prayer. He recognised that God was the Only One who could help in times such as these – and God is the Only One that can help you too!

Fully rely on God, and you will be amazed at how quickly things can suddenly turn around. Look to God for His strength; do not rely on your own for it will fail you. Ask Him for His wisdom as you face this battle together. He will help you, if you ask him. Remember - you are not alone!

Almighty God, I look to You, I rely on You to deliver me from this extremely difficult situation, which you know all about. Please strengthen me and give me everything I need to go through this. With your hand in mine, I can face tomorrow! Amen.

08 MAY

There for You

2 Chronicles 15 v 4: But in their distress they turned to the LORD, the God of Israel, and sought him, and he was found by them.

What is the first thing we usually do when we are distressed? We tend to complain a lot and talk about our problem over and over again, getting ourselves more and more upset and therefore even more distressed than we were in the first place! Instead, if only we would turn to the Lord we would save ourselves a lot of needless stress and tension.

Turning to the Lord in our distress will instantly calm us – as we change our focus from our problem to Him. He promises to be there for us if we turn to Him. If we take the time to be still and listen - he will speak to us with words of Wisdom that will instantly bring us the 'peace' we so desperately need.

O Lord, you know of my every distress – you know and understand me and you know exactly how to help me. Please forgive me for forgetting you and for allowing myself to get so upset. Thank you for being there for me; may I turn to you whenever I am in distress. Amen.

09 MAY

Keep Going!

2 Chronicles 15 v 7: But as for you, be strong and do not give up, for your work will be rewarded.

Does it sometimes feel as though you've come up against a brick wall? Despite your best efforts you seem to be getting nowhere? At times like this, it is easy to be tempted to just 'throw in the towel' and give up. But God has promised that if you keep on going - you will be rewarded for your labour.

Whenever things get tough, don't give up – keep pressing on through the difficulties and the apparent unproductive phases of your life, and you will eventually reap a harvest – bearing much fruit!

So, keep on doing what you have been doing and be strong in the Lord. This is God's word for you today - Keep going!

Thank you Father for your Word for me today, I really needed this. I need to press on and not give up. Please strengthen me so that I can keep on going and I trust I will be rewarded in your perfect time. Amen.

10 MAY

How Deep is Your Love?

2 Chronicles 15 v 16: King Asa also deposed his grandmother Maacah from her position as queen mother, because she had made a repulsive Asherah pole. Asa cut the pole down, broke it up and burned it...

Such is King Asa's love and passion for God that he destroys the idols in the land including his own grandmother's Asherah pole! Asa understands just how detestable these idols are to God, and his love for God far outweighs any concern he may have about upsetting his grandmother; he even deposes her from her position in the Royal Household – that's how serious this is!

As I read this, it made me wonder about my own love for God – is it deep enough for me to risk upsetting someone in order to do what God is asking of me? Do I love God more than man? Do I love God more than my family? We all need to ask ourselves these questions from time to time.

O Lord, please stir within me a greater love and passion for You, so that, like King Asa, I will not want any idol (object, person or desire) to come before You in my life. Please reveal any idols I may have. Amen.

11 MAY

Missed Opportunity

2 Chronicles 16 v 12: ... Though his disease was severe, even in his illness he did not seek help from the LORD, but only from the physicians.

Can this really be the same man we looked at yesterday? – King Asa? Sadly, it is! In his later years, at a time of war, he turned to the King of Aram for help instead of to his God, and now in his illness he only turns to physicians, therefore missing out on the help he could otherwise have received.

I wonder; how many of us do the same thing? Do we forget that God is our helper and healer? How many missed opportunities for His help and healing in our lives have we had? Our God is the same today – he can still help and deliver us, and heal us too. All we need to do is ask Him! So why not ask him right now - and face no further missed opportunities?

O Heavenly Father, may I not become like King Asa, who no longer relied on you, but turned only to man for his help. May I be ever conscious of my need of you and even now I ask you to come to my aid, in Jesus' name. Amen.

12 MAY

Spread the Word

2 Chronicles 17 v 9: They taught throughout Judah, taking with them the Book of the Law of the LORD; they went round to all the towns of Judah and taught the people.

Unless we read or hear God's Word we are not going to know it, and therefore we are unlikely to put it into practice.

King Jehosaphat knew the importance of sharing God's Word with everyone, so he sent out his officials and certain Levites to all the towns in Judah to teach the people God's Law. No town was to be left out.

We need to hear good biblical teaching on a regular basis; it is for our benefit, for as we learn more about God, so we get to know Him! We all need this for our growth and development as believers, so that we are not ignorant of God's ways and can then, in turn, teach others.

Is God calling you to Go and spread His Word today?

Thank you Lord for leaving us with your precious Word. I long to receive more of it so that I know you better and in turn may go and share it with others. Amen.

13 MAY

Our Eyes Are on You

2 Chronicles 20 v 12: O our God, will you not judge them? For we have no power to face this vast army that is attacking us. We do not know what to do, but our eyes are upon you.

Are you facing an extremely difficult challenge or situation? Are there major decisions to be made, but you have no idea what to do? Is it all beyond your ability to deal with? Then today's word is for you!

Turn to God and ask him for His strategy, His Way forward – look to Him and He will give you everything you need. He will show you what to do. He may well use other people to do this, but let him know that your eyes are firmly fixed on Him for the answer! Then be on the lookout for His intervention. He may not do what you expect – but it will all work out for your ultimate good. So, look to God and Trust Him with the outcome.

My eyes are on you Lord, and I thank you for this reminder today. I look to You, and Trust You with the eventual outcome in my current situation. Amen.

14 MAY

It's His Battle

2 Chronicles 20 v 15: … This is what the LORD says to you: "Do not be afraid or discouraged because of this vast army. For the battle is not yours, but God's."

However hard the enemy is pressing in against you, never lose sight of what God is saying to you. It becomes so easy to panic when coming under attack and then, in our panic, we tend to forget God and can no longer hear His Voice – just when we so desperately need to.

We forget that the battle belongs to the Lord, and so we often struggle, in our own strength, trying to sort things out. God will fight for us if we will let him. There is no need to be frightened if we know our Heavenly Father has everything under control – just like a child is no longer frightened of the local bully if he has his father by his side.

So, if you are facing a battle today, don't be discouraged – God will fight for you!

O Father, may I be at 'peace' just like the little boy facing the local bully who has his father by his side; because I have you by my side and you will protect me and fight for me. Amen.

15 MAY

Apron Strings

2 Chronicles 22 v 3: He too walked in the ways of the house of Ahab, for his mother encouraged him in doing wrong.

Ahaziah was only 22 years old when he became King and he made such a bad job of it that he was only on the throne for one year! His problem was that he was still very much under his mother's influence – he took his lead from her rather than from the Lord.

If you want to follow God, make sure you have Godly people in your life to influence you for good. You may need to get away from some people if they are a bad influence on you or draining the life out of you. This may include your mother if you feel as an adult you are still very much under her control – cut the apron strings! You need to be free to be the person God made you to be. Let Him be your guide through life – He needs to come first.

Please open my eyes today Lord and show me anyone in my life that is having a bad or negative influence on me. May you then give me the strength and wisdom I need to withdraw from their influence, even if that person happens to be my mother! Amen.

16 MAY

The Secret of Success

2 Chronicles 26 v 5: He sought God during the days of Zechariah, who instructed him in the fear of God. As long as he sought the LORD, God gave him success.

There are numerous books you can find on how to be successful in life, with lots of advice on how to get yourself up the ladder of success. But only one thing is needed, and that is for us to seek the Lord in everything we do!

If we truly fear God, that is, respect his views and want to follow his ways and please him, we will want him to guide us through our life at every turn so that we are doing His will and not our own. We will then have the security that everything is going to work out well for us.

However, if we decide to be in charge of our own lives - making our own plans without reference to God's will at all, then there is no guarantee of how things will work out for us Not that we seek the Lord to be successful; we seek him because we love and fear Him and want to bring Him glory. Success is simply a by-product of us following the Lord.

Heavenly Father, thank you that it is You who gives us true success in life and may I always remember that. Amen.

17 MAY

A Good Clear Out!

2 Chronicles 29 v 16: ... They brought out to the courtyard of the LORD's temple everything unclean that they found in the temple of the LORD. The Levites took it and carried it out to the Kidron Valley.

If God's temple needed to be cleansed from everything that was not meant to be there, things that defiled it, then how much more do we, as God's temple, need to be cleansed from all that defiles us?

God knows we are far from perfect, apart from Jesus, and yet he still accepts us just as we are. However, his desire has always been for us, to get rid of those things within us that are harming us and others, and hindering our walk with him. Don't you desire that for those you love?

Our heavenly Father lovingly deals with us and brings things to light; it's a life-long process and we need to co-operate with him each time he reveals something new to us that needs dealing with. Allow him to do the inner cleansing that you need.

O Lord, I don't want anything inside me that shouldn't be there. Please reveal those things to me and help me have a good clear out! Amen.

18 MAY

First Things First

Ezra 3 v 3: Despite their fear of the peoples around them, they built the altar on its foundation and sacrificed burnt offerings on it to the LORD, both the morning and evening sacrifices.

I wonder, do we sometimes forget the importance of worship? I am challenging myself with this very question today!

Picture the scene - the exiles have just returned to Jerusalem, which is now in ruins, and are surrounded by potential enemies, and yet even in their fear they get out there and start building the altar (place of worship) first, before they begin on the temple (see verse 6)! So, they are out there in the open - exposed and vulnerable to attack, but worshipping their God comes first – before anything else. So great was their love for their God!

Do we let the fear of man prevent us from worshipping God before everything else in our lives? How important is worshipping God, to you?

O Heavenly Father, please help me to have such a passion for you that my first thoughts always turn towards worshipping you! Amen.

19 MAY

Beware of the Enemy's Work!

Ezra 4 v 4-5: Then the peoples around them set out to discourage the people of Judah and make them afraid to go on building. They hired counsellors to work against them and frustrate their plans...

Let's take a look at how the enemies of Judah tried to prevent them from continuing with the work. They tried to: 1) Discourage them; 2) Instil fear in them, and; 3) Frustrate their plans. Similar tactics are still being used today, whenever God's work is undertaken.

Maybe someone reading this right now is struggling to continue with the work the Lord has given them? Don't let the enemy win. Cry out to God and He will strengthen your arm to continue. Don't be intimidated. If God has given you a task to do He will help you accomplish it, whatever it may be.

Thank you so much Lord for making me aware of the enemy's tactics. Help me to recognise these at the onset and to redirect any negative thoughts before they take hold. Whenever I face opposition, may I lean into You for everything I need to resist it. Amen.

20 MAY

God Can Change Hearts

Ezra 6 v 22: ... the LORD had filled them with joy by changing the attitude of the King of Assyria, so that he assisted them in the work on the house of God, the God of Israel.

The Israelites have finished rebuilding the temple, so you would expect that alone to bring them great joy – but why does it say they are filled with joy? They are full of Joy because God had changed the heart of the King, so that he helped them rather than hindered them with the work.

Do you believe God can change people's attitudes? There is a saying, 'A leopard can't change its spots' - well no, 'it' can't, but God Can!

People are often the cause of some of our greatest problems in life, and if we try to change them, we will soon create an even bigger problem on top! But if we turn to God and ask Him to change them – well then we are in with a chance! God can change a heart to one of favour rather than antagonism, to love rather than hate and to peace rather than strife!

O Lord, may I remember to ask you to change people's hearts rather than trying to do so myself. Amen.

21 MAY

Opposition

Nehemiah 4 v 1: When Sanballat heard that we were rebuilding the wall, he became angry and was greatly incensed. He ridiculed the Jews...

Whenever we try to move forward with God, we are highly likely to face some form of opposition. We have an enemy who does not want us to make any kind of progress in our faith. So don't be surprised when this happens – the fact that it does is a sign that you are doing God's will. I have just this minute been interrupted by a 'pop up' on my laptop – a very subtle means of distraction maybe – but a great illustration of what I am talking about!

We can use such opposition to spur us on to continue with the work, just as the Jews did when rebuilding the wall of Jerusalem. They didn't let Sanballat's ridicule of them hinder them; they prayed to God for his intervention in the situation and continued on with the task at hand.

May I encourage you today, if you are being opposed in any way for doing what God has asked you to do – then take heart – it is a sign you are doing the right thing and that God will enable you to finish what you have begun.

Father God, thank you for showing me how to look at opposition in a positive light. Thank you that you are on my side, so I have no need to fear. Amen.

22 MAY

Be Prepared

Nehemiah 4 v 17-18: ... Those who carried materials did their work with one hand and held a weapon in the other, and each of the builders wore his sword at his side as he worked.

Today we will look at how we can best prepare ourselves against any potential attacks. We can see in the above verses that the Jews were taking no chances! They were continuing on with the work but also had some very practical protection in place!

What protection do we have available for us today? What did the Jews do? First, they prayed, and then they made sure they had their swords ready at hand. Prayer is still our first means of defence and then, like the Jews, we too have our swords – God's Word. We can speak God's Word into and over the situation in which we find ourselves, and then we can take any practical steps that may be necessary.

We must not allow the enemy to cause us to cower and draw back from the work we are undertaking. Maybe you are in this very situation today – don't let the enemy win, take heart and carry on, for God is with you!

O Lord, please help me when I come under attack and feel like giving up – remind me to pray to You and use your Word, knowing that you will sustain me. Amen.

23 MAY

Now Strengthen My Hands

Nehemiah 6 v 9: They were all trying to frighten us, thinking, "Their hands will get too weak for the work, and it will not be completed." But I prayed, "Now strengthen my hands."

Fear has an amazing way of making us feel weak; legs that can usually stand firm and strong suddenly turn to jelly and we feel as though the life has been sucked out of us; we have no energy at all. This is why the Jews were being lied about and intimidated (two of the enemy's traits) to make them incapable of building the wall.

Nehemiah was fully aware of what was going on and knew exactly what to do when feeling physically weak – he called on the strength of his God!

Are you feeling weak and at the end of yourself today? Well, if you are that's good, because now you can be completely full of God's mighty strength if you will ask him to take over. He will strengthen you in your work, so that your hands are anointed for the task. Even you will be amazed at how quickly and well the work gets completed.

Thank you Lord, that in my times of weakness - You are my strength! Nothing is impossible with you. I shall not lack, for you give me all the strength that I need. Amen.

24 MAY

The Joy of the Lord

Nehemiah 8 v 10: Nehemiah said, "Go and enjoy choice food and sweet drinks, and send some to those who have nothing prepared. This day is sacred to our Lord. Do not grieve, for the joy of the LORD is your strength."

The Jews were commanded to celebrate and to no longer grieve, for they had been crying as they heard the word of the law being read, all realising how far from God they had turned. But God didn't want them to remain sad; he wanted them to experience His joy. They were told that the joy of the Lord was their strength - and it is your strength too!

Yesterday we saw how easily fear can sap our strength, and today we can see that if we lose our joy in the Lord, we will ultimately lose our strength too! It all makes sense now why so many of us find ourselves battling with feelings of depression - the devil knows that if he can take our joy from us, then he can also steal our strength!

It is not the Lord's will for us to be downcast and feeling sad – he wants us to experience the fullness of His joy; the joy that only he can give us! Our God is for us and not against us!

O Lord, please help me turn to you and receive your joy; the joy that comes from knowing you and from being in your presence. Amen.

25 MAY

For Such a Time as This

Esther 4 v 14: ... And who knows but that you have come to royal position for such a time as this?

Queen Esther had been shown great favour and had been chosen from among many other young girls to become queen. And now when her own people are destined to be destroyed by the king's edict (he did not know she was a Jew), Esther is the only person who has any chance to plead with him for their lives because of her position as his wife!

Let me ask you a question. "Where has God positioned you?" Maybe you feel frustrated with where you are? But God has placed you there, and he has placed you there for a reason. Take a look around and view things through God's eyes and you will begin to see why he has put you there! This may be where you work or go to school, where you live, or the church you attend; or any other place that you regularly go to, or anything you are regularly involved in. Ask God to show you for what purpose you are there? Don't despise where God has placed you, embrace it; for who knows, maybe you are there for such a time as this?

Thank you Lord for encouraging me today! I feel quite excited at the prospect of finding out what you have for me to do in the places where you have positioned me! Please show me Lord! Amen.

26 MAY

Fasting Power

Esther 4 v 16: ... Do not eat or drink for three days, night or day. I and my maids will fast as you do. When this is done, I will go to the king, even though it is against the law. And if I perish, I perish.

Before going to see the king, Esther knows that she needs all the help she can get and so she calls for all the Jews in Susa to fast along with herself and her maids! It is a matter of life and death, and fasting shows how serious they are in entreating God for his help.

Whatever your views on fasting might be, may I encourage you to view it as a very helpful discipline, sadly one that is very much neglected in our times. Maybe we would see far more answers to our prayers if we were willing to fast when we pray. I will leave that with you to ponder.

As a result of Esther's request for a three day fast, the king holds out the golden sceptre to her when she approaches, and so she lives and is able to help her fellow Jews by saving them all from destruction!

Father God, you are pleased to see how serious we are when we pray and sometimes fasting is a necessity; please may I be willing to do this when you ask me to. Amen.

27 MAY

Reap What You Sow

Esther 7 v 10: So they hanged Hayman on the gallows he had prepared for Mordecai.

Hayman was the man responsible for the edict to destroy all the Jews! He despised Mordecai because he had refused to worship him. He became so furious with Mordecai that he even built a huge gallows on which to hang him.

However, Esther was very wise and asked Hayman to dine with her and the king before she revealed to the king that Hayman was the man responsible for the order to destroy all her people. The king is absolutely furious and orders that Hayman be hung on his very own gallows.

Hayman had only, the previous evening, been boasting about how favoured he was; but now how the tables have turned. What he had sown – the destruction of life - was now being fully reaped by himself.

May we learn a big lesson here - be very careful what you sow! For whatever we give out will come back on us, either good or bad!

O Heavenly Father, please forgive me for the times I've been so full of myself that I've failed to notice the bad seed I've sown into people's lives. Help me to do only good to my fellow man. Amen.

28 MAY

God Is in Control

Job 1 v 12: The LORD said to Satan, "Very well then; everything he has is in your hands, but on the man himself do not lay a finger."

No matter how bad things may look in our lives and however much it makes us think God no longer cares for us and has deserted us, when we read today's text we can plainly see that God IS firmly in control of what is allowed to happen to us, and if God has allowed it, then we can be sure that he has a plan and purpose for it, even though we may never realise what it was for.

We may not understand it and may even find it impossible to equate with a loving God – but be assured that God knows exactly what he is doing. He will only allow things to come upon us that we can bear, with His help, and that will ultimately work out for good.

O Lord God, you are my Father and I thank you that you are in control of all that happens to me. Any bad things that you allow to occur in my life, I believe occur for a reason and that you can use all of them to bring about good. Please help me whenever I doubt this Lord; help me to really trust you in all circumstances. Amen.

29 MAY

God Is Sovereign

Job 1 v 21: ... The LORD gave and the LORD has taken away; may the name of the LORD be praised.

What an example Job is to us today! When he lost everything he had, including his ten children, he continued to praise God just as he always had! I wonder how many of us would find that possible?

We bring nothing with us into this world and we take nothing out; all we have comes from God, by his grace. And just as the Lord gives, so he can take away.

In today's world this is particularly hard to hear. We expect all our needs to be met instantly, and having brought God down to our level, we can treat him pretty much like a vending machine (only wanting what we can get out of him), rather than as who he really is – our Sovereign Lord and God

Please forgive me Lord if I have lost sight of who you really are – A Sovereign God! You are at complete liberty to both give and take away, but one thing never changes – you are still God and worthy of my praise – whatever the situation.
Amen.

30 MAY

Beware of What You Dread

Job 3 v 25: What I feared has come upon me; what I dreaded has happened to me.

It is a well-known fact that the mind has great power, even over our own bodies. If only we realised just how much our 'thought life' affects our day-to-day life, we would be far more careful about what we allowed ourselves to think about.

As in the case of Job, if we keep on fearing and dreading certain things happening to us – we will more than likely find these very things actually occurring in our lives.

This verse has personally helped me a lot; whenever I now find myself dreading something, I remind myself of what Job said and this brings me up sharp and encourages me to think of something positive instead, and motivates me to stop dreading the very thing I don't want to happen.

Thank you Lord, for the way your Word can speak right into our lives and guide us – even in our 'thought life'. Please help me not to dread things and to look towards you whenever fears threaten to attack my mind. Amen.

31 MAY

This Too Shall Pass

Job 11 v 16: You will surely forget your trouble, recalling it only as waters gone by.

These words are so true, but when we are in the midst of the storms of life it can be very hard to imagine that calmer waters lay ahead. Job could not have suffered much more, but eventually his troubles came to an end and so will yours!

Take heart today if you find yourself in the midst of troubled waters; these words are for you - "This storm will pass, calmer seas are just ahead. Keep pressing through and don't give up hope, for God is with you and will help you get through this."

We are each on a journey, and sometimes we need to travel through difficult terrain – but we keep our eyes on our final destination, knowing that eventually we will arrive, for however difficult the journey gets, we know we are just passing through!

O Father, thank you that you brought Job safely through and out to the other side of his trials and I thank you that you will bring me out too, in Jesus' name. Amen.

01 JUNE

In the Gap

Job 16 v 19-21: Even now my witness is in heaven; my advocate is on high. My intercessor is my friend as my eyes pour out tears to God; on behalf of a man he pleads with God as a man pleads for his friend.

Despite his dreadful suffering, Job has amazing spiritual and prophetic insight. In this verse, he is speaking of having an advocate in heaven to stand in the gap for him and plead his case. He is actually describing 'Jesus', who has not yet come into the world. Despite his pain, Job remains connected to God, confident that his case is being upheld in heaven.

Now this was the very thing that Satan was trying to do – take away Job's security in God, and he tries to do the very same thing to you – to make you doubt God's love for you by sending troubles, trials and temptations into your life. But like Job, we too have an advocate – someone to stand in the gap for us – his name is Jesus.

O Lord, thank you for opening up this knowledge to me today. Suddenly it all makes sense. May I always remember that however tough life gets I have someone interceding for me in heaven, someone who cares about me, no matter what. Amen.

02 JUNE

Self-Destruction!

Job 18 v 4: You who tear yourself to pieces in your anger…

Just as harbouring un-forgiveness will do more harm to us than to the person we hold things against, so too will any unresolved anger! Anger, when not properly dealt with tends to get pushed down within us and can often result in depression later on. Our souls can become filled with such bitterness and rage that physical symptoms will manifest in various forms of ill health.

We are only harming ourselves by holding on to these negative emotions. Choose 'Today' to hand over any that you have. Choose 'Today' to give it all to God; make a clean break with any unresolved anger and release God's healing power into your life.

Ask God to search and cleanse your heart so that you can live in the fullness of life that he has for you.

Heavenly Father please forgive me for holding on to my anger – people have hurt me and I have felt justified in doing so, but you tell me to forgive and let go; and so I do right now. I give it all to you Lord, every last bit and I thank you for taking it away, in Jesus' name. Amen.

03 JUNE

Face to Face

Job 19 v 27: I myself will see him with my own eyes – I, and not another. How my heart yearns within me!

Again, Job is uttering prophetic words in the midst of his agony! Never let your pain stop you from being used by God. Job firmly believes that after he dies he will see God. This is utterly amazing, as Job is seeing this before Jesus has come into the world to show us the way to heaven. What faith he has!

Doesn't this give you great hope? Life can throw the worst at us, but no one can take away our future hope of living with our Heavenly Father forever after we die. We who truly believe, like Job, will see God 'face to face'! Job yearned for this very thing and our hearts should do so too!

O Father, how I look forward to being with you for eternity.
No words can describe my joy and excitement at the prospect
of seeing you face to face - how I long for that day to come!
Until then, please protect me on my life's journey; may
nothing lead me astray or divert me off my pathway 'home' to
you. Amen.

04 JUNE

Precious Treasure

Job 22 v 22: Accept instruction from his mouth and lay up his words in your heart.

If we only listen to God's words but don't really accept them or treasure them deep in our hearts, if we rebel against God's instructions and don't hold on to them we will soon find ourselves in trouble.

God speaks to us for many reasons – to warn us and guide us, to encourage us and sometimes chastise us. We need it all, because God knows what we need and when, and if we store up His words within, we can turn to them in a time of crisis. We can speak His Word out during our times of temptation, or any other distressing situation we may find ourselves in, and we must carry out anything that God tells us to do. His Word is trustworthy and true and is there for our ultimate good.

Thank you Lord for the power of Your Word. Help me to treasure it deep within my heart, that it may become so much a part of me, that it is part of who I am. May I follow your directions and draw on your Word in troubled times. Amen.

05 JUNE

Truly Tested

Job 23 v 10: But he knows the way that I take; when he has tested me, I shall come forth as gold.

What makes Job's words so amazing here is that he spoke them while in agony! He had the insight to know that God was with him and that God had allowed all these bad things to happen to him, in order to test his faith. Job firmly believed that once he'd gone through this furnace of affliction, he would come out as gold. In other words, it would all have been worth it - he would come out much the better for it!

I wonder if there is someone reading this today and you are at the end of your tether due to all the bad things that have been happening to you. If so – be encouraged - God knows where you are and what you are going through and he will use even your bad experiences to transform and strengthen your faith. Trust Him to bring you through this. He has you in his hands.

Thank you Father for showing me that my tough times in life can have a purpose – please bring me forth as 'gold', that I in turn may help others going through tough times and give you all the glory. Amen.

06 JUNE

Someone to 'Hear' Me

Job 31 v 35: Oh, that I had someone to hear me!

When experiencing extreme pain we can feel very alone and rather cut off from normal everyday life. The cry of our heart will often be: 'If only I had someone to really understand what I am going through and how I am feeling'.

Job's friends sadly let him down rather badly, just when he needed them most. Does it remind you of anyone else's experience? The bible is full of friends letting down friends, just look at what happened to Jesus. In his hour of greatest need, all his friends deserted him, one betrayed him and another denied even knowing him!

But the good news is that - we do have someone who 'hears' us; someone who knows us better than we know ourselves – we have God! We can share everything with Him. God is always there, waiting for you with open ears!

Thank you so much Lord, that you are always there, ready to really listen to me. Help me to remember to turn to You when I need someone to understand me; and please remind me to share all my concerns with you. Amen.

07 JUNE

God Speaks

Job 33 v 14: For God does speak - now one way, now another – though man may not perceive it.

It is true – our God speaks! God speaks to us continually through his creation, but sadly today most people just don't hear him or even believe that he exists.

God can speak to us in many different ways, but unless we are open to hearing from him we will miss it. He can speak to us through other people, through a song, through an event in our lives and most often through His Word.

God also longs to speak directly into our hearts; but in order to hear Him we will need to be still, not just physically but also mentally. We will need to calm our thoughts and still our minds, especially in this day and age when there is so much to distract us. It won't be easy and will take some time and self-discipline, but it will be so worth it in the end – when we finally get to hear what God wants to say to us personally!

O Lord my God, thank you so much that you desire to speak to me - may my ears be open to 'hear'! Help me to regularly practice being still before you, so that I may hear your voice. I ask this in Jesus' name. Amen.

08 JUNE

My Rescuer

Job 36 v 16: He is wooing you from the jaws of distress to a spacious place free from restriction...

This is God's heart for you – to see you set free from the trap you are heading into – from the distress the enemy has planned for your life. God wants to woo you back to himself, to bring you out into a spacious place, a place of freedom, free from restriction. Sound good?

Are these words speaking directly into your situation today? If so, allow God to woo you. It may mean letting go of some things or people that you would rather hang on to, but anything God asks you to give up was only doing you 'harm' anyway. Trust Him – He knows what is best for you. Let God woo you today.

Once you have been rescued from those jaws of distress you will never look back – what joy and delight you will find in that spacious place – free from restriction!

O Father, how can I thank you enough? Thank you for seeing the danger set before me – for being my rescuer and for wanting to woo me back to you. Please release me from the enemy's trap! Amen.

09 JUNE

Beyond Understanding

Job 36 v 26: How great is God – beyond our understanding!
The number of his years is past finding out.

Who can say that they understand God? Do we even realise just how great He is? I only have to look into the universe and I am lost already; my mind cannot grasp the vastness of it all, let alone the vastness of God, who is even that much bigger again!

If we could understand God then he wouldn't be God! He is way beyond anything we can imagine with our finite minds. This is what causes us to be in awe of Him and is why we worship Him so - our God is Awesome!

Let us take time out to ponder all that God has made and how he has planned it all with such intricate detail. How could such detail be the result of an accident? Then there are all the wonders and miracles he has performed since creation – for he is God, and He can do anything!

I worship and praise you O Lord our God - for who you are
and for all you have done. There is no-one else like you – you
are beyond understanding. Amen.

10 JUNE

There's No Stopping God

Job 42 v 2: I know that you can do all things; no plan of yours can be thwarted.

At the end of Job's test he firmly believes that God can do all things and that nothing can stand in the way of God's plans. What a comfort that must have been after all he had gone through.

Whatever God sets out to perform, will be accomplished - nothing can prevent it - for if God has said it, then God will do it! Opposition may well come against it, but it will not prevail because God already has the victory. He knows the end from the beginning and he will bring to pass all that he has promised. I believe that is a Word for someone today.

God will have His way – never doubt it!

Heavenly Father, thank you that nothing is impossible with you, and whatever you have promised in your Word – that, you will carry out. I thank and praise you that nothing can stop your plans O Lord. Amen.

11 JUNE

A Real Eye Opener

Job 42 v 5: My ears had heard of you but now my eyes have seen you.

At the end of Job's time of testing he suddenly sees God as he really is – far bigger than he could ever imagine! He realises that he hadn't really known God like he thought he had. When the penny finally drops, Job despises himself and repents in dust and ashes - humbling himself before his God. And it is then that God blesses Job's life even more than he had blessed it before!

We may think we know God well – but do we really? I challenge myself with this question. I believe we would do far better if we said we will never fully know God but that each day we hope to know him a little better than the day before – we will not run out of days, I promise you! This will keep us humble, with a real awe of who God is and a deep desire to know him even more.

Dear Lord, thank you for this real eye opener today. Please forgive me if I have been making presumptions about knowing you when I still have so much more to learn! You are so much greater than any image of you we can ever conjure up. Praise your Holy Name! Amen.

12 JUNE

Social Distancing

Psalm 1 v 1: Blessed is the man who does not walk in the counsel of the wicked or stand in the way of sinners or sit in the seat of mockers.

Today's verse warns us to watch the company we keep! The progression here - from walking, to standing, to sitting - implies a subtle and gradual increase in how much we become influenced. At work, you hear your colleagues running down the boss or criticising the company you work for. The more time you spend with these colleagues, the more you socialise with them, the greater effect their negative words will have on you - even to the point where you are highly likely to join in with them. Now sadly, you have lost your credibility as a Christian!

So, if you want to be blessed today – take heed of the psalmist's words and steer well clear of being sucked into the ways of the world. This may mean socially distancing yourself from certain people or even giving up some friendships if they are having a negative impact on you.

O Lord, please forgive me if I have allowed myself to be badly influenced by ungodly people or friends. Please help me to stand out and be different from the crowd – for then I will be truly blessed. Amen.

13 JUNE

Sleep in Heavenly Peace

Psalm 4 v 8: I will lie down and sleep in peace, for you alone, O LORD, make me dwell in safety.

When anxiety is running high and adrenaline is pumping through our body it can, understandably, be very difficult to relax enough to sleep. However, here at the end of Psalm 4 we have this promise - we can indeed lie down and sleep in peace, because we can hand everything over to our God, knowing that he will keep us safe.

The key here is to let go of all that is troubling us before we attempt to settle down to sleep, and once we have given it all to God, we need to trust that he will take care of us until the morning. If we meditate on God's promises to us and allow him to minister to us, we will indeed sleep in 'peace' – for He is our peace!

Heavenly Father, please remind me to pray to you before I go to bed each night and to hand everything over before I settle down to sleep. I believe you alone can give me this 'peace' that I so desperately need right now. Thank you Father. Amen.

14 JUNE

A Fresh Start

Psalm 5 v 3: In the morning, O LORD, you hear my voice; in the morning I lay my requests before you and wait in expectation.

What better way is there to start your day than by laying all your requests before God, knowing that he has heard you?

'I'm not a morning person', you may say, but whenever your day begins it's always good to start it by talking to your Heavenly Father, even if it is while you are doing other things like getting ready for work. It is really beneficial to take the time each morning to lay the events of your day before the Lord and to let him know specifically what you need for this day!

You know it makes sense, so why not try it and wait expectantly to see what God will do with your day and what a difference it will make?

Somehow Lord, I find myself feeling quite excited at the prospect of trying this each morning! Thank you Lord that You will be there waiting for me at the start of each new day – ready to hear my requests! Help me to remember to talk to You before my day gets under way. Amen.

15 JUNE

People Pleasing

Psalm 12 v 2: Everyone lies to his neighbour; their flattering lips speak with deception.

You may have read this verse today and thought, 'No way is that true', but if we examine it more closely, I think you will agree with me that this occurs far more often than we realise.

If we are honest, we all want people to like us and think well of us and without realising it we often find ourselves complimenting those people that we want to impress. We praise them for things that actually we don't really think are that great, and we do things to keep them happy, even though our heart isn't in it at all. Are these not 'lies'?

Because we want people to like us, we go overboard trying to please them and yet the only person we should be concerned about pleasing is the Lord our God.

Thank you so much Lord for making me aware today of the subtleness of lying and my tendency to want to look good in the eyes of others by buying their friendship with flattery! I am so ashamed; please forgive me Father, and may You be the person I most want to please in my life. Amen.

16 JUNE

Unstable Props

Psalm 16 v 4: The sorrows of those will increase who run after other gods.

I wonder, what or who do you turn to in a time of crisis? Do you maybe phone a friend, grab a bottle of wine or reach for the chocolate? Or maybe you turn to pornography, gambling or illegal drugs? Doing any of these things is equivalent to us running after other 'gods', and none of them will help you in the long term; they will all ultimately let you down.

I sense I am speaking to someone today who desperately needs to hear this word – many of your sorrows are a direct result of you looking for help and satisfaction in all the wrong places. God is the only one, true and stable prop that you will ever need – He will never let you down! So why not turn to Him today, instead of running after your other gods? In fact, why not make today the day that you hand everything over to him and begin afresh?

Thank you O Lord, for showing me the dangers of running after other gods instead of You - the true and living God. Please forgive me for doing this, and today I draw a line in the sand and choose to turn away from these other gods and turn back to You. I trust and believe that you are all I need to hold me up. Amen.

17 JUNE

With God's Help

Psalm 18 v 29: With your help I can advance against a troop; with my God I can scale a wall.

Wow, what a powerful word this is; with God's help we can come against and conquer things that are so much bigger than we are.

I wonder, are you facing such a situation today? If you are, then this is God's word for you! With His help you will get through this challenge, however impossible it may seem to you. Naturally speaking it may well be impossible, but take heart, for God is with you to help you.

If you're not facing anything difficult today, then next time you are, remember to turn to God for help as He wants you to be dependent on Him for everything! So often we struggle because we are trying to do what only God can do.

Thank you that you are a Mighty God – strong enough to help us, in all our conquests and battles. With you we can do the seemingly impossible! Help me remember to ask for your help Lord. Amen.

18 JUNE

On Cloud Nine!

Psalm 19 v 1: The heavens declare the glory of God; the skies proclaim the work of his hands.

I really feel this verse could do with some added photographs to show just how amazing God's universe really is and how beautiful the skies can be in such a variety of ways! Each morning we awake to see God's handiwork and, generally speaking, it leads us to be in awe of His glory!

God can be clearly seen in all His creation, but sadly many don't recognise whose handiwork it is they are looking at. If you want to feel close to God, then just spend some time gazing up at the stars or a glorious sunset or stunning cloud formation. I promise you, it will make you realise just how BIG and amazing our God is! Why not take some time out this week to do just that.

O Father, when I look to the skies my heart just soars as I think of the one who created such beauty. Thank you Lord for giving us such a visible sign of Your Glory! Cause us to think of you each time we look up at the beautiful heavens that you have made. Amen.

19 JUNE

I Will Trust

Psalm 23 v 4: Even though I walk through the valley of the shadow of death, I will fear no evil, for you are with me...

Although this verse is probably one of the most well known and most often quoted, do we really believe it for our own lives? Anxiety has become an increasing problem in our world today, even among Christians, and so maybe we haven't fully grasped what this verse is saying?

I am writing this during the outbreak of Covid-19, a time when many of us are literally living in the valley of the shadow of death! Can we really have no fear at a time like this? What causes David to say he will not fear? It is the fact that the Lord is with him and just as God was with David, so is he with you! Think about it - Jesus promised to be with us to the very end of the age, and if we truly believed this we wouldn't be afraid, because we would know that He is with us, protecting us – for that is what a Shepherd does!

May I see you Lord as my Shepherd - caring for me at every turn, especially today as I walk through this valley may I know your presence with me. Amen.

20 JUNE

You Will Sing Again

Psalm 30 v 5: ... weeping may remain for a night, but rejoicing comes in the morning.

Whenever you are going through a time of sorrow, whatever the cause may be, this verse gives us the assurance that it will eventually come to an end and you will be able to sing again! It may not end the very next morning, but it will end.

It is the hope of better times ahead that can keep us going through a difficult time. There is a time to weep and a time to laugh and we need to let our grief run its natural course – there are no shortcuts through our pathway of pain. There is a healing work in our tears as we release our sorrow; little by little we are healed within. Don't try to rush through grief – give all your tears and pain to God and allow him to bring you through the night and into the glorious morning – when you can rejoice once again!

Father God I thank you, that as my Loving Father I can come to You with all my sorrow and pain and that you will take my tears and heal me from deep within. Thank you that you will restore to me the Joy I once had. Amen.

21 JUNE

Our Perfect Guide

Psalm 32 v 8: I will instruct you and teach you in the way you should go; I will counsel you and watch over you.

I don't know how good you are at making decisions, but I do know we would all benefit greatly if we remembered to seek the Lord's guidance before making one! This is true for both large and small decisions as they are all just as important in the Lord's sight, although maybe not to us.

This verse emphasises just how involved the Lord wants to be in our lives and it should bring us great joy and comfort, knowing that He will guide us and watch over us in all we do – but we need to let him!

If you are about to make a decision, then I encourage you to hand it all over to the Lord and then wait for His guidance – He will instruct you and show you in His good and perfect time! You may need to exercise some patience, but if God is leading you, then you can be sure of a good outcome!

I thank and praise you Lord for your promise to teach me and show me the way ahead. Thank you that you will be there to lead me and guide me through all my decision making, both now and in the future! Amen.

22 JUNE

Our Heart's Desire

Psalm 37 v 4: Delight yourself in the LORD and he will give you the desires of your heart.

When I first came across this verse I took it to mean that if I took the time to enjoy the Lord's company, in return he would grant me all those things I really, really wanted. I am not sure if that's how you see it too? Well, in more recent times I have come to see it in a completely different way.

I now read this verse as saying that, as I come into and enjoy the Lord's presence - really delighting in Him as a person – He will fulfil my heart's desire, my need to be treasured, loved, cared for and valued. In other words, He is the answer to all my desires – He becomes my one desire!

A question for you – which of the two versions excites you the most? Which one resonates with you? Your answer will reveal your true heart!

Please forgive me Father, if I am more excited about getting what I want rather than what you want to give me. Thank you for showing me another meaning to this verse today – may I continue to ponder it. Amen.

23 JUNE

Don't Fret

Psalm 37 v 8: Refrain from anger and turn from wrath; do not fret – it leads only to evil.

Anger is an emotion, and one that we cannot help but feel from time to time, and usually for a very valid reason. The feelings of anger themselves are not a sin, but it's what we do with those feelings that matters - allowing them to completely take over so that we begin to act out of them is wrong, and even just fretting over something can easily escalate into full blown rage.

What happens when we get really angry? First our blood pressure starts to rise and then we are highly likely to start saying an awful lot of bad things that we will later regret. Cursing and swearing are never far away and in some cases violence may well break out! If there is no opportunity to take it out on a person or object, our anger can turn inwards leading to resentment, bitterness, unforgiveness and later depression. So now you can see why the psalmist is telling us to refrain from anger.

O Lord, please help me to control my anger in its early stages, before it gets out of hand. If I can sense it starting to rise within me, please remind me at this point to come to you and hand it all over. Amen.

24 JUNE

Out of the Pit

Psalm 40 v 2: He lifted me out of the slimy pit, out of the mud and mire; he set my feet on a rock and gave me a firm place to stand.

Have you ever reached a point in your life where you felt you couldn't get any lower? Even those fortunate enough to have never suffered with depression, have more than likely gone through some tough times.

The description of the slimy pit is a pretty good one, of how it feels to be in the depth of depression - there is just no way up or out of there! Maybe you can relate only too well to this; you feel trapped and alone and if you try to get out you find yourself slipping back down again - hence the slime! It's also a pretty good description of a bad addiction.

On your own you are helpless; but God sees you, he looks down from above, has mercy on you and pulls you up and out of the slimy pit of depression or addiction – as only he can! And then he makes you stand firm on the rock that - is Jesus! Ask him today, to rescue you.

Have mercy on me O Lord, rescue me from this pit of destruction; set me free to serve and worship You. Amen.

25 JUNE

Talk to Yourself!

Psalm 42 v 5: Why are you downcast, O my soul? Why so disturbed within me? Put your hope in God, for I will yet praise him, my Saviour and my God.

The word 'downcast' describes the position of a sheep that has fallen onto its back and cannot get up again. When you're feeling low and troubled, your soul is very much like the poor downcast sheep - it needs to put its hope in its Shepherd coming to save it!

In today's psalm we find the psalmist talking to himself as he encourages himself to put his hope in God, because he knows that his 'true' hope comes only from God, for he has promised to give us a hope and a future and beyond that - eternal life with Him!

The psalmist also says that he will praise his Saviour and his God, which is such a good piece of advice, as it automatically takes our mind away from our problems and focuses our mind onto our Lord and Saviour, who is the only one who can really help us!

O Lord, I am putting all of my hope in you. I praise and thank you that you are always there to help me get back on my feet again; I just need to remind myself! Amen.

26 JUNE

Be Still

Psalm 46 v 10: Be still, and know that I am God...

These may be very familiar words to you, but have you ever stopped to think about what they really mean? In the context of this psalm the Lord is commanding his people to stop – to stop fighting! This gives it quite a different meaning as it really emphasises the need to be still – to stop what we are doing and to stop what we are thinking about too! Unless we do both of these things first, we won't get to know God as he really is, because we won't sense His presence or hear His voice.

When our thoughts are troubling us or we are on the daily treadmill of life, we can so easily forget that God is still there with us and that he is still in control of everything. He wants us to take time out – to stop what we are doing, to be still before him, to let all of our striving cease. Then we can be still in his presence, that precious place where we will know that he is God! Why not try it right now?

Here I am O Lord, I choose now to stop everything, to stop the whirring in my mind, to quiet my soul before you and wait for you here. Amen.

27 JUNE

A Pure Heart

Psalm 51 v 10: Create in me a pure heart, O God, and renew a steadfast spirit within me.

Do you ever long for your heart to be pure, just as David did in this psalm? He wrote this after his sin of adultery, and murder was brought to his attention by Nathan the prophet. David never wanted to fall into sin like that, ever again; so he asked God to make his heart pure and his spirit steadfast!

Maybe you feel your heart is already pure; but for those of us who don't, may we cry out, just like David did, and ask the Lord to give us a pure heart. If you are feeling bad today over some things you have done wrong, turn away from them now and ask God to change your heart and to renew a right spirit within you, so that you can live wholeheartedly for your Lord, and do those things which he has prepared in advance for you to do.

O Lord, how I long for my heart to be pure! Please cleanse me from all that is impure! Create in me a pure heart today and make me steadfast as I follow you; please don't let me fall from your grace. Amen.

28 JUNE

Cast Your Cares

Psalm 55 v 22: Cast your cares on the LORD and he will sustain you...

Have you ever been on a hike and got to the point where your backpack is feeling so unbearably heavy that you just can't go on? Well, going through life carrying all our worries and concerns is a very similar experience, and we may suddenly find we can no longer cope with it all. Now, if someone steps in and offers to carry your backpack you can then continue with the hike; and the same is true in life. If someone offered to carry all your burdens you would feel free again and be able to cope with the demands of everyday life!

Well, God has stepped in to carry your load – all you need to do is hand it all over to Him – why carry it any longer? Now imagine that weight being slowly lifted off of your shoulders; how light do you feel now? God is taking care of all your burdens and He will sustain you on the rest of your journey.

Please forgive me Father for struggling on, trying to take care of everything myself. I choose this day to hand all my cares and worries over to you, to let you carry them for me as I continue to walk on – so much lighter! Amen.

29 JUNE

Under Your Wings

Psalm 57 v 1: ... I will take refuge in the shadow of your wings until the disaster has passed.

O what an amazing peace, what a feeling of love, warmth, comfort and absolute security! That is a description of how it feels when we rest under the shadow of God's almighty wings. This place of refuge is freely available to all of us if we choose to take it, if we run to the Lord during our troubled times. What better place is there to be?

Although this is figurative, in the Spirit it is exactly where we can be, even in the midst of disaster; but we need to make the effort to get there by giving up our panic and turning to God. He is there waiting for you and longing for you to run underneath his wings and receive all his love and comfort at this time.

O Lord, I choose to let go of the panic that is engulfing me, and I run to You. I place myself under the shadow of your wings, under your love, care and protection. Thank you Lord, what better place could I be? Amen.

30 JUNE

Pray for Protection

Psalm 64 v 1: Hear me, O God, as I voice my complaint; protect my life from the threat of the enemy.

We may not have an actual physical enemy as David did, but we all have a spiritual enemy called Satan, who works against us from without and within.

One of his cleverest tricks is to set us up and, without us realising it, we fall headlong into his pre-arranged trap! When things are causing you to lose your peace – guess who set them up? The answer is to quickly turn to the Lord and tell him of your problem and cry out for him to protect you from the devil's schemes.

We need to remember to pray for protection, not just for ourselves but for our families and loved ones too! We cannot afford to become complacent otherwise the enemy will walk all over us and seriously attempt to destroy our faith.

Please protect me and all those I love from the threat of the enemy. Thank you for the reminder to do this Lord. Please guard and protect me from falling into those traps that the evil one sets for me. Thank you! Amen.

01 JULY

A Cry for Help

Psalm 69 v 15: Do not let the floodwaters engulf me or the depths swallow me up or the pit close its mouth over me.

As you read these powerful and descriptive words of David, can you feel how absolutely desperate his situation was? I found myself right there with him as I read them!

'All we can do is pray.' Have you ever heard people say that, almost as a kind of last resort? But the opposite is so true - we should be crying out to our God right from the very onset of any potential disaster.

Sometimes God will allow desperate situations to occur in our lives, whether they be physical or mental (David's words are a pretty good description of depression); both are equally traumatic. God wants us to turn to Him - to cry out to Him for help and turn our focus away from the bad situation, whatever it may be, and onto Him! When in need - cry out!

O God, please come to my rescue! I need You - only you can save me from this horrendous mess I am in right now. Please come to my aid quickly! Amen.

02 JULY

Shaken but Not Stirred

Psalm 75 v 3: When the earth and all its people quake, it is I who hold its pillars firm.

Does it feel like everything in your life is being shaken right now? Does one bad thing after another seem to be happening to you? Are you feeling anxious over world events? We all go through these periods of shaking from time to time.

In today's psalm we have this assurance from God that He is the one who holds everything in place – firm and secure. If we remember this fact during the whirlwinds of life, then just like the storm we can be completely calm within the centre of our being – shaken but not stirred!

Our Father wants us to trust that he is in control of our life and holds everything in His hands so we needn't fear the storm when it comes, but remain calm and at peace with Him.

O Lord, please help me to trust you more; help me to find rest in You within the centre of the storm, knowing that you are holding everything steady for me. Amen.

03 JULY

Remember

Psalm 77 v 11: I will remember the deeds of the LORD; yes, I will remember your miracles of long ago.

The psalmist pens this verse whilst going through something very traumatic. Despite his pain and suffering he chooses to focus on the goodness of God and does so by remembering all the things that God has done in the past and the amazing miracles He has performed. The psalmist is encouraging himself by reminding himself that God can do anything and if he has done it before he can surely do it again and can come to his aid right now.

I wonder, do you need encouraging today, by remembering all the things that the Lord has done for you? Even if your life is relatively calm right now, remembering what the Lord has done for you is always a good thing to do, as it not only encourages you and lifts your spirits, but it also strengthens your faith.

You might find it helpful to write out a list of all that God has done for you; I think you will be amazed at how doing this builds you up and increases your joy!

I thank and praise you Lord for all the great things you have done for me. Amen.

04 JULY

Yearning for God's Presence

Psalm 84 v 2: My soul yearns, even faints, for the courts of the LORD...

How wonderful it is to enter into a place of worship, where heaven comes down and we dwell with God, with no distractions to spoil this most precious time. It is the nearest experience to being in heaven that we can have while still here on earth. Time just seems to stand still during those special moments - when all you are aware of is God's presence, nothing else matters!

Have you ever had that experience? If not, would you like to? Or maybe you haven't experienced it for a long time and, just like the psalmist, you are yearning even now to come into that place of true worship again?

Nothing else compares to being in close fellowship with our Lord; you don't want this moment to ever end. You just want to enjoy His presence forever – which of course one day we will!

O Lord, today you have stirred up a real desire in me to come into your presence far more often than I do. Why, O why do I stay away for so long when deep down my heart is longing for you? Here I am Lord - I come! Amen.

05 JULY

Teach Me Your Way

Psalm 86 v 11: Teach me your way, O LORD, and I will walk in your truth; give me an undivided heart, that I may fear your name.

It is so easy to come under pressure from other peoples' opinions and ideas about things so that, without realising it, we may find ourselves wandering off course - off God's pathway of Truth!

The way to ensure we stay on God's perfect path for us is to have our own integrity, and not to follow someone else's morality. The more we read and study God's word then the more we will know and understand his ways, and in turn be able to follow him more closely. In a nutshell, we need to fear God more, regardless of what other people may say or think of us.

Heavenly Father, please help me to find more time to look into and study your word, so that I may know and understand the way you would have me go in life. I only want to follow you Lord; please help me resist the temptation to follow others and give me an undivided heart. Amen.

06 JULY

Where Are You God?

Psalm 88 v 18: You have taken my companions and loved ones from me; the darkness is my closest friend.

Have you ever felt absolutely alone? Although you may know in your head that God is with you, in your actual experience you cannot sense him being remotely near you at all. You have lost so much and really need to feel comforted by God's presence – but you cannot find Him. It is as though he has left you just when you need him the most.

I love the psalms because they are so real – the psalmists pour out their hearts and tell it like it is, yet they always come around to realising that God is there with them and is for them!

Why not try writing your own Psalm to God? God wants us to be real with him and this is one way in which we can be; tell Him what's on your heart right now - just as it is!

Forgive me Lord when I don't understand your ways; help me to be honest with you and tell you exactly how I am feeling - for you know anyway. Amen.

07 JULY

His Work through Us

Psalm 90 v 17: May the favour of the Lord our God rest upon us; establish the work of our hands for us – yes, establish the work of our hands.

What a brilliant verse this would be to speak over our forthcoming day! All too often we rush headlong into a new day, with all that we have to do, and get stuck in without stopping to ask God to help us, and then we wonder why we end up with problems.

Why not take this verse as a daily prayer for your life? If it helps, maybe write it out and stick it somewhere you will see it each morning before your day gets underway. Try this and see what a difference it makes to your days and how much easier and more successful the work of your hands becomes. Be bold and ask God for his favour to be upon you today!

Forgive me Father for rushing into each day without asking for your help. I want to change this – starting today. Please come into my everyday working life; may you grant me your favour and establish the works of my hands, for your glory Lord. Amen.

08 JULY

Never Too Old

Psalm 92 v 14: They will still bear fruit in old age, they will stay fresh and green...

God loves us all: full stop. Whether we're a new born baby or someone in our nineties or beyond. Sadly though, 'the world' doesn't see things in quite the same way. To be accepted in this world you need to be a certain way, but in God's Kingdom things are very different. God loves and accepts us just as we are, including those of us who would consider ourselves to have reached old age. One day we will all become old, and when we do, we will want to be loved and treated in just the same way as everyone else.

If you happen to be someone who is older, may you know this today – God has not finished with you, you are not too old for God to use, and he will continue to do so until you join him in heaven. So be encouraged - in God you will never grow old!

O Heavenly Father, I thank you that you love us all equally, no matter what our age. In Your kingdom there is no age difference – we are all the same in your sight and of equal importance to you! Amen.

09 JULY

Don't Panic!

Psalm 94 v 19: When anxiety was great within me, your consolation brought joy to my soul.

Despite having overwhelming feelings of panic rising from deep within you, seemingly out of your control, there is a way to turn your panic into peace! Maybe that sounds completely impossible to you? But please believe me when I say that it isn't!

If you begin to focus your attention on God rather than on the cause of your anxiety and allow him to minister to you through prayer and the reading of His Word, you will begin to feel yourself automatically calming down. Choose to deliberately rest yourself in His presence, and allow Him to gently comfort you and give you His peace.

What joy and release this will bring to your troubled soul, setting you free from the chains of anxiety. Praise God!

O how can I thank you enough Lord? Now I know how to deal with anxiety - whenever I feel it beginning to rise within me I can turn straight away to You for comfort and peace. Amen.

10 JULY

We Bow Down

Psalm 95 v 6: Come, let us bow down in worship, let us kneel before the LORD our Maker…

There is a time to dance and cheer, to wave our hands in the air in Praise of our God, but there is also a time to bow down in reverence and awe and worship Him,

Just hearing the words 'bow down' brings a sense of humility with it; O how we need this humility in our worship today! It is during these most precious moments of true worship, where not only are our bodies bowed down but also our hearts, that we find ourselves completely overwhelmed by God's presence, and who wouldn't want that?

I challenge you today, to come and bow down before the Lord your maker, allow yourself to become low, so low that you can really and truly worship Him for who He is! He is so deserving of our worship.

Please humble me this day I pray O Lord, bring me to my knees, that I may truly worship you for who You are and for all you do. I love you Lord. Amen.

11 JULY

I Am His

Psalm 100 v 3: Know that the LORD is God. It is he who made us, and we are his; we are his people, the sheep of his pasture.

Have you ever really stopped to think about that before? We are His! Pause and think about it for a moment - You belong to God, You are His personal possession! How did that make you feel?

Knowing this fact should make us feel very secure, knowing that we belong to God, the creator of the whole universe!

Maybe today this is all you should do – spend your time thinking about your relationship with God, thinking about what it means to be HIS! Ponder on how a shepherd cares for His sheep, how he will do anything for them – how God will do anything for you!

It has been so good just to stop today and to really think about the fact that I belong to You - My God. Thank you so much.
Amen.

12 JULY

Clean Sweep

Psalm 103 v 12: ... as far as the east is from the west, so far has he removed our transgressions from us.

East and West never meet and that is why once our sins have been forgiven by the Lord, these sins will never be met again! God removes them totally, not partially; he makes a clean sweep of them, never to be seen or remembered again and gives us a fresh start! Satan, on the other hand, wants to keep on reminding us about what we did wrong! Sound familiar?

If God can forget our sins, choosing to remember them no more, removing them completely from us – then why can't we do the same? Sadly all too often we listen to the enemy's lies, or we allow our guilt to consume us. Thinking we know better than God is a form of pride. We may think it's good to be feeling sorry and beating ourselves up over our sin – but if God has forgiven us then who are we to continue to feel bad about it? God says to you today, "Forgive yourself and let it go!"

O Heavenly Father, I choose today to forgive myself and to stop looking back over my past sins and mistakes. Thank you so much for removing them so far from me that I am now set free from all my guilt. Amen.

13 JULY

Where You're Meant to Be

Psalm 107 v 30: They were glad when it grew calm, and he guided them to their desired haven.

Before we reach our desired destination we may well have to go through a storm or two in order to get there; but we have God with us, helping us to get through them!

If you find yourself in dangerous waters and far from where you would like to be in life, then I encourage you to cry out to God – for He alone can calm your troubled sea. Not only will he see you through this difficult time, but he will also make sure you reach the place you desire to get to – the place you are meant to be!

Isn't it comforting to know that on our journey through life, however tough or challenging it gets, we are never alone – we have God with us, leading and guiding us all along the way?

Please take my hand Lord and guide me to the place I am supposed to be. May I be confident that you will ensure my safety as I travel through the storms of life. Thank you Lord, I trust in and rely on you. Amen.

14 JULY

Give God All the Glory

Psalm 115 v 1: Not to us, O LORD, not to us but to your name be the glory, because of your love and faithfulness.

I don't know about you, but I still struggle to remember not to take the credit for what God has done through me. This becomes especially hard when people are praising you for something you have done, but you know it was all of God. If you do the right thing and give God all the glory, it often appears to those who are praising you that you are practising false humility and unable to accept praise; so you have yourself quite a dilemma!

When we choose to take all the praise and glory for ourselves – God is not pleased, because he is God and He deserves All the Praise and All the Glory! Without him we wouldn't be able to achieve anything of any real worth or value in this life. We should be so grateful to God for all He is doing through us that we should be the first one to give him all the praise!

May all the glory go to you, O Lord, may all the glory go to you; for you are worthy of all our honour and praise. Help us remember, O Lord, that without You, we can do nothing!
Amen.

15 JULY

Rejoice Whatever

Psalm 118 v 24: This is the day the LORD has made; let us rejoice and be glad in it.

Isn't it so much easier to rejoice on those days when the sun is shining, the skies are blue and the birds are singing; or when you have something really exciting to look forward to? Whatever the day ahead may bring us, it is still the day that the Lord has made!

We can rejoice because we have been given this new day as a gift and we need to view it as a fresh start with new opportunities to show kindness to others. Each day we can rejoice in our God and thank him for all he has done for us and for all that he is going to do today!

All it takes is a new perspective. If we look at each new day in positive ways, whatever else is going on we can handle it, knowing that God is there with us helping us through because He has made this day and already knows exactly what's in store.

Thank you Lord, I praise and thank you for this new day; may I rejoice in it and eagerly await your guidance through it! Help me do this each morning. Amen.

16 JULY

Your Wonderful Word

Psalm 119 v 18: Open my eyes that I may see wonderful things in your law.

O the wonder and the beauty that is contained within the Word of the Lord; such is the treasure hidden within its pages that before turning one of them over, it is well worth speaking out this verse as a prayer!

Make today's verse your prayer and continue to make it your prayer before reading the Word, it will make your bible reading time so much more exciting. You will always come to it in anticipation of what the Lord has for you - what does he want to say to you, what does he want to teach you, what does he want to show you? Can you already feel your spirit rising in response?

Today I want to stop and thank you Father, for all that is contained within Your Word; for the rich treasures stored there just waiting for me to discover. Suddenly, bible reading has become alive with excitement for me and I long for you to open my eyes so that I may see wonderful things in your law. Your word is so precious to me; may I not take it for granted but approach it in the anticipation of receiving all that you desire to teach me. Amen.

17 JULY

Guiding Light

Psalm 119 v 105: Your word is a lamp to my feet and a light for my path.

If you've ever been out at night where there are no street lights, you will know how difficult it is to find your way, and how easy it is to stumble or fall over a piece of uneven pathway because you cannot see clearly where you are going! If we attempt to make our journey through this life without any reference to God's word, we will soon find ourselves in a similar predicament – stumbling about, unable to see where we are going!

As we read God's word it guides us and shows us the way ahead. It helps us not to travel down any blind alleys as we follow the light it gives us. Spending time in God's word draws us closer to God and teaches us what He wants us to do, and where He wants us to go. So if you find yourself in a dark place and cannot see your way out of it, turn to God's word and it will bring illumination!

Thank you Lord for showing me how much I need your word as it is vital for my life's journey; may I turn to it regularly. Amen.

18 JULY

Surrounded by You

Psalm 125 v 2: As the mountains surround Jerusalem, so the LORD surrounds his people both now and for evermore.

Do you ever feel vulnerable, or lost and alone? Take a moment now to picture the mountains surrounding Jerusalem. Whichever way you look, there they are - firm solid and mighty - all around you! Now imagine instead that God is there surrounding you, no matter where you look – He is there all around you. How does that make you feel? - Loved? Safe? Secure? Protected? That is exactly how we should feel all the time, because as it says in today's verse – He surrounds us both now and for evermore!

Make a conscious effort to live each day with this fact in mind - God is surrounding you, he is everywhere you are. You cannot escape his love and care; it will transform your life!

O Lord, may I meditate on this verse until it becomes a reality in my life. Thank you that you are all around me, that I am surrounded by your love, care and protection. This brings me such an amazing sense of peace and calm, I really can't thank you enough. Amen.

19 JULY

Why Work in Vain?

Psalm 127 v 1: Unless the LORD builds the house, its builders labour in vain.

Why are we talking about building houses you may wonder? This verse is a great analogy to warn us against the folly of starting a project of any sort without first consulting God and receiving both the plan and directions from Him.

It can be so easy to think of a good project to set up without making any reference to our Lord, but we do so at our peril. If it hasn't come from God we will find ourselves struggling; there will be no real joy in it for us and at the end of the day it will go nowhere. We will have wasted all our time, effort and energy for no good purpose.

Seek God's plan before you take on anything new and check with Him it is something he wants you to be involved with – it will save you needless amounts of stress.

*Thank you Heavenly Father for this stark warning today –
may I apply it to my life in every way. Thank you that you only
want what is right and best for me. Amen.*

20 JULY

The Blessings of Unity

Psalm 133 v 1: How good and pleasant it is when brothers live together in unity!

We've probably all heard of 'sibling rivalry' but sadly, all too often, we find it among our Christian brothers and sisters within the church! This should not be. What kind of example are we showing those who live outside God's kingdom? It doesn't look pretty, or indeed, very Christ-like! And it causes us to be far more vulnerable to enemy attacks.

However, when brothers and sisters agree and get along well together without any infighting, what a great witness to outsiders we are and we will experience God's full and rich blessings upon us. Then we can stand strong against our enemies, leaving no chinks in our armour.

So, make every effort to live in harmony with each other, for we are all responsible for our part and we need to play it well - making every effort to live in peace.

O please help us Lord, to represent you well. Help us to keep the strife out of our lives, may we keep the bond of peace between us at all times. Amen.

21 JULY

Give Thanks!

Psalm 136 v 1: Give thanks to the LORD, for he is good. His love endures for ever.

This one verse is repeated so many times in God's word that it needs to be taken note of. Remembering to give thanks to God is so important, because it immediately takes our focus away from our problems and onto God. Being thankful and saying so will automatically lift our spirit.

Straight away this verse gives us two things to thank God for; first that He is good and secondly His love is everlasting - it will never run dry. Everything else in our life won't always be good and other people's love may well run out for us; but God is different from everything and everyone we know. He is to be thanked throughout our lives, with our being ever grateful for all He is!

Change the way you think today. Whatever you are doing – stop, and give God all the thanks he deserves!

Forgive me, O Lord - I so often take you for granted. Thank you that I can rely on You when all else becomes bad in my life. You alone are good and when others let me down - You still love me. Amen.

22 JULY

God Made Me and Knows Me

Psalm 139 v 13: For you created my inmost being; you knit me together in my mother's womb.

I am who I am because of the way that God has made me, and he knew all about me, in minute detail, before I ever took my first breath or gave my first cry – isn't that mind blowing!

No one knows you better than your heavenly Father. He knew you existed before your earthly parents did; he even knew what you were experiencing within your mother's womb. He saw your unformed body developing in the secret place. You are fearfully and wonderfully made – pause and think about that…

Only your Maker truly understands you; He knows you better than you know yourself. He created and designed you to fulfil a specific purpose. God has a far better plan for your life than you could ever imagine.

O Lord, may I never lose sight of how wonderfully I was made. Thank you that you have always been with me, from before I was even born! Thank you that you know everything I've ever been through – even from within my mother's womb - and all I am going to do in the future. Amen.

23 JULY

Keep My Mouth Shut

Psalm 141 v 3: Set a guard over my mouth, O LORD; keep watch over the door of my lips.

Have you ever said something and immediately known that you should have kept quiet? Once our words are out, they are out and we cannot take them back, however much we may want to or however much we may apologise for them.

How we all need to pray this prayer, along with the psalmist. Words come so easily into our minds and the journey to our mouth is very short. Words are so powerful – either for evil or for good. With our tongues we can tear someone apart, leaving them feeling completely broken or we can build someone up by encouraging them and complimenting them, leaving them feeling confident and happy. I know which words I would rather receive, but why is it I so often say the wrong words to others?

Father God, each day may I surrender my mouth to You, so that it may be used for Your glory, rather than to run others down or to moan and groan about life. Please put a guard over my lips and stop any wrong thoughts I may have from travelling out of my mouth. Amen.

24 JULY

Sleep on It

Psalm 143 v 8: Let the morning bring me word of your unfailing love, for I have put my trust in you. Show me the way I should go, for to you I lift up my soul.

Sometimes it gets too late in the day to do anything about an urgent decision or situation in your life. Rather than tossing and turning all night worrying about it, wondering what you should do, why not place it all in God's hands – trusting him to come through for you in the morning?

Today's verse is a brilliant verse to pray before going to sleep. It releases you from the pressure to decide now, it allows you to hand everything over and to even feel excited about what God is going to do and where he is going to lead you. Now you can sleep on it. What a relief that is!

Thank you Lord for this word today, it has completely transformed how I will go to bed each night. I will give all my concerns to You - trusting you with them and looking forward to all you are going to do in not allowing my problems to disturb my night's sleep. Amen.

25 JULY

Forever Praise You

Psalm 145 v 2: Every day I will praise you and extol your name for ever and ever.

How can I not praise you Lord, after all you've done for me? How can I not extol your name when you are the Lord and Creator of the Universe? You deserve Praise and Honour and Glory for all eternity!

You are the only true God, there is no other like You; all others are false. You have always been and always will be; your Kingdom never ends. It is good to praise you O Lord!

I lift my voice and tell of your wonders, things too marvellous to fully comprehend. You alone deserve my Praise; you alone are Holy and Exalted above the earth; you alone Reign in Majesty, overseeing your Kingdom from on high.

O Lord, my God, how my heart soars as I Praise You May you be pleased with this song that arises from within; may my heart continually be in awe of you - longing to Praise your Name! Amen.

26 JULY

Sweet Healer

Psalm 147 v 3: He heals the broken-hearted and binds up their wounds.

God knows your hurt, he knows your pain, even though you may hide it from those around you. God knows, and more than that he completely understands.

This word is for someone today. God is looking right into your heart right now and he is weeping with you whilst holding your hand – can you not sense his presence? He is sitting right there beside you, just longing to comfort you and remove your pain. As he wipes the tears from your eyes, he offers you His sweet and gentle healing balm. Allow Him to minister to you deep within. As you sit in His presence, allow him to take it all from you - allow Him to do the work that only He can do. He will fill those empty places with His love and joy; you will be amazed at how different you feel.

Heavenly Father, I thank you so much for coming to me as 'Healer' today. I give you all my pain and anguish and ask you to take it Lord - all of it! Come and fill me with your love again and bring back the joy I once knew. Amen.

27 JULY

Do Good

Proverbs 3 v 27: Do not withhold good from those who deserve it, when it is in your power to act.

This is a very challenging verse, if taken seriously, as there are people in desperate need all around us. However, alongside this command we will also need to hear God's voice directing us in what to do and for whom to do it.

May I encourage you to be open to hearing the Lord's voice guiding you – being extra sensitive to those inner nudges from his Holy Spirit. He will show you both how and where you can 'do good' for others, as he lays people and situations on your heart.

Their needs will vary – they may simply require some advice, or at the other extreme you might need to part with a large sum of money in order to help them out in a crisis. Maybe they need a good friend, a listening ear, some practical help or some prayer.

O Lord, I thank you so much for drawing my attention to this verse today Please may you keep it to the forefront of my mind and make me extra sensitive to the leading and guiding of your Holy Spirit, that I may joyfully obey your call and do good to those in need. Amen.

28 JULY

Wise Up!

Proverbs 13 v 10: Pride only breeds quarrels, but wisdom is found in those who take advice.

When we argue with someone, we will each have our own point of view and think that we are right and the other person wrong. We will enjoy airing our opinions and putting the other person's down – but who's to say that we are right? What good comes from a quarrel?

Our pride gets us into an awful lot of trouble! We would save ourselves and others a lot of needless upset and stress if we took the time to listen to the good advice found in today's verse.

Next time you feel a quarrel about to start – Stop, and listen to the advice that's coming up from within your own heart - don't let it take place, don't let pride lead you astray.

Thank you God for revealing to me the root cause of my quarrelling – pride - which is me thinking I am right and have all the correct opinions on a matter. Please forgive me and help me to wise up and take heed of this great advice to stop quarrelling. Amen.

29 JULY
Good Medicine

Proverbs 14 v 30: A heart at peace gives life to the body, but envy rots the bones.

If we find ourselves continually envying what other people have, either their gifting or their possessions, and resenting them as a result, we will automatically lose our peace, as we will no longer be satisfied with what God has given us. We will, instead, be in a constant state of angst and striving to improve our lot. If we continue to put our bodies through this stressful state then it will begin to have a serious knock-on effect to our health.

Envy may, on the surface, not seem such a bad thing – but the fact that it not only steals our peace but can also make our bodies sick shows us just how dangerous it can be. Our loving heavenly Father knows all this and that is why he tells us not to envy others or what others have, but instead, to be content with what we have and what he has gifted us to do.

O Lord, it is so easy to become envious today, when we can so readily compare our lives to others on social media. Please help us to stop Lord, and give you thanks for all that we have. Amen.

30 JULY

Gentle Power

Proverbs 15 v 1: A gentle answer turns away wrath, but a harsh word stirs up anger.

I have to confess I grew up thinking you had to shout if you wanted to be heard, but I have since observed the power of a gentle voice tone, and have found this to be particularly valuable in calming situations, especially when looking after young children.

I have witnessed the two extremes - a parent desperately shouting at their child but with no effect, and a mother whispering to her daughter and gaining her full attention and co-operation. Please don't get me wrong, I'm in no way passing judgement here. Parenting is one of the hardest jobs out there, but when I discovered this 'gentle power' I was immensely grateful, and have found it to be very helpful because it can save so many volatile situations from getting out of hand.

Thank you Lord for the great wisdom that's found in your Word. Today's verse is such a powerful one as it can change the whole course of a situation in which we find ourselves. Please help me to remember this the next time I am faced with someone's anger - may I remember to respond in a calm and gentle way. Amen.

31 JULY

Secure in His Name

Proverbs 18 v 10: The name of the LORD is a strong tower; the righteous run to it and are safe.

If you find yourself feeling vulnerable, afraid or under direct attack then know this; there is a place where you can be kept completely safe from harm, but you need to do something first – you need to run there!

God's name is so powerful, and we can often forget that His name provides us with protection. As we proclaim that name we are safe in Him, but we need to remember to place ourselves under his protection.

If you find yourself immobilised by fear then just cry out the Lord's name, recognising that He is your answer in this current situation. Imagine yourself running into that high tower - your security is in His Name!

Thank you Lord for the power of Your Name, nothing and no one can stand against it. Please remind me of this Father, and to use it for my protection next time I am in a dangerous or distressing situation. Praise your name! Amen.

01 AUGUST

The Lord Will Intervene

Proverbs 20 v 22: Do not say, "I'll pay you back for this wrong!" Wait for the LORD, and he will deliver you.

As tempting as it may be, when someone hurts you badly, to retaliate and get your own back by causing them pain in return, it is never the right thing to do and will most likely lead to even more pain for you. This teaching is most challenging, because with every fibre of our being we want to defend ourselves, and make the other person pay for what they did to us. However, if we just press the pause button for a moment, step back and hand the whole situation over to God, he will, in His time and His way, step in and sort everything out on our behalf and you will be amazed at how everything pans out for your good.

Maybe you are in this very situation today? If so, the Lord is saying to you – "Come to Me, I understand exactly how you are feeling. I have seen all that has happened to you and I will deal with the person who has hurt you – Trust Me!"

Please help me Lord, I am still so tempted to get my own back. Instil in my heart the knowledge that I can leave it all to you, knowing that you will come through for me. Help me trust you in this. Amen.

02 AUGUST

Get a Grip!

Proverbs 25 v 28: Like a city whose walls are broken down is a man who lacks self-control.

What a great analogy this is for warning us of the dangers of not having self-control. Maybe we can trace back some of our major problems in life to a time where we didn't control ourselves?

When a city has no walls it is wide open to enemy attack, it is left completely exposed and unprotected! We too will be in this state if we live in a reckless manner - following our own natural instincts and urges, without making any effort to control them.

Self-control will protect us, not only from being led into sin, but because we have resisted temptation we will be in a stronger position to be kept safe from enemy attack. Sadly God cannot do this one for you, although he can certainly help, but the bottom line is, and this may sound harsh - we need to get a grip and control ourselves.

O Heavenly Father, thank you for showing me how important having self-control is. I confess I find this very difficult at times and often fail you; please help me by the power of your Spirit, in Jesus' name. Amen.

03 AUGUST

A Friend Indeed

Proverbs 27 v 17: As iron sharpens iron, so one man sharpens another.

We all need friends, and a true and loyal friend can be very hard to find. As Christians we also need to have a Christian friend with whom we can share our deepest concerns and burdens, praying together about them and building up and encouraging each other too!

A 'true' friend will be totally honest with you and tell you when they see you going astray or doing something wrong; friends like this are extremely hard to find! Most friends will only ever flatter you, because they are afraid of upsetting you, but we really need to hear the truth, and 'sharpening' needs to take place within our friendships. We need to be accountable to each other, and who could do it better than a friend who only ever wants what is best for you? To be sharpened may sound rather painful, but we all need to be made sharp, so that we can be useful. Let us welcome it next time we are corrected by a true friend.

O Lord, please find me friends that will be open and honest with me and that I may in turn be open and honest with them – true friends indeed! Amen.

04 AUGUST

Perfect Timing

Ecclesiastes 3 v 1: There is a time for everything, and a season for every activity under heaven...

God has made a time for everything and it is wise for us to follow his timing in our lives rather than trying to force things on ourselves!

Let's take a butterfly for example. When emerging from its chrysalis there is a real struggle involved as it tries to get out, and if we saw it we may be tempted to help – but if we did it would never fly and soon die as a result. The time of struggle is needed for the butterfly to strengthen its wings, so it needs to emerge in God's perfect timing in order to live!

What a lesson for us this is - in so many ways! It reminds us that we need to be in awe of God's perfect timing, for He alone knows all the ins and outs of our circumstances and He alone knows just the right time for everything to occur in our lives

O Heavenly Father, please forgive me whenever I try to run ahead of you or lag behind. You know the best time for everything to take place and with that in mind please help me to stay in tune with your will for my life. Amen.

05 AUGUST

Live for Today

Ecclesiastes 7 v10: Do not say, "Why were the old days better than these?" For it is not wise to ask such questions.

Sometimes looking back can be beneficial for us, especially if we are recalling all the amazing things that the Lord has done for us. But there can also be a tendency to look at the past through rose-tinted glasses, and to believe that everything was better back in 'the good old days'!

Today's verse tells us that it isn't wise for us to compare the past to now. Why? Because we need to live our life for Today! Our reality is here and now, the past is in the past and to a great extent needs to stay there. If we keep comparing our life to how it used to be, we will become permanently dissatisfied with our lot, and that is not how God wants us to live.

If I am talking to someone today who has a problem with this – please make today the day you stop and begin to live your life again - in the here and now!

O Lord, I am sorry if I have been living in the past, instead of here with you right now. Please forgive me and help me change; with your help I can live for today! Amen.

06 AUGUST

Moderation in All Things

Ecclesiastes 7 v 18: ... The man who fears God will avoid all extremes.

I have heard it said that when you take things to the extreme you're playing right in the devil's playground! Satan loves it equally if you eat too much or hardly eat at all and he loves it if you talk too much or you barely talk at all; he loves it if you spend all your money or you barely spend at all and he loves it if you sleep all day or hardly sleep at all.

Watch out for extremes! These are just a few examples, but they show how going to the extreme can be bad for you. Even good things like work can be overdone so we need to have balance in our lives - a time for rest and leisure as well as work, and as Christians we also need time set aside to be with God, to feed our spirits. As soon as we get out of balance in any area of our lives we are asking for trouble!

O Lord my God, please help me to fear you and avoid all extremes in my life. Please remind me if I start to get out of balance in any area of my life. Amen.

07 AUGUST

Go For It!

Ecclesiastes 11 v 4: Whoever watches the wind will not plant; whoever looks at the clouds will not reap.

Do you tend to put things off, waiting for everything to be just perfect before you finally go for it? Chances are that if you do that you will never get around to it, and will therefore be robbed of many blessings!

Instead of looking at the circumstances and waiting for them to change – try looking to God and seeking His direction and guidance for when to go for it. This will transform your life and help you lead a far more productive one.

Is there something you are putting off doing today? Have you been getting those little nudges from the Holy Spirit as you have been reading this? If so - go for it!

I am so sorry Lord for all my dithering, for being too slow to act and making excuses for not stepping out or acting sooner. May I remember to seek your face and take my lead from you Lord, rather than continually looking at the conditions all around me. Amen.

08 AUGUST

Whose Agenda?

Song of Songs 1 v 6: ... My mother's sons were angry with me and made me take care of the vineyards; my own vineyard I have neglected.

Sometimes we may find ourselves living by someone else's agenda rather than our own; doing what 'they' want rather than what we should be doing! Nevertheless, we may be unaware that this is what's happening.

We all have things for which we are responsible; things that we should be doing whether it's cleaning the house, going to work or spending time with our family. A danger signal for us will be when we find we have little time for these things or we are no longer putting in our full effort. We then need to take a look at our life and take stock of what we are doing and why. Are we busy fulfilling somebody else's agenda rather than our own? Our own responsibilities should come first; no one should be controlling us to the extent that these are being neglected.

Please help me to be strong enough to say 'no' to the wrong demands that others place upon me, especially when they are causing me to neglect the work and responsibilities that you have given me Lord. Please make me aware of when this is occurring. Amen.

09 AUGUST

Unquenchable Love

Song of Songs 8 v 7: Many waters cannot quench love; rivers cannot wash it away.

The word 'love' is so often used in the wrong way that it can now mean little more than a fleeting fancy. Love has become a feeling rather than a life-long commitment to someone.

Genuine love is priceless; there is nothing better than to be truly loved for who we are and by someone that always has our best interests at heart. Human love can sometimes be this strong, but the only love fully guaranteed to never let us go is God's love! Whatever you go through in life God will always be there for you, continuing to love you, no matter what!

Nothing can wash away God's love from you, no matter how great the storm, and knowing this fact should bring us such love, joy, peace and security.

O Heavenly Father, I am overwhelmed when I realise the truth of your love, the depth of your love and the reliability of your love for me. Why do I ever doubt you? Please forgive me, and thank you for loving me. Amen.

10 AUGUST

Willing Volunteer

Isaiah 6 v 8: Then I heard the voice of the Lord saying, "Whom shall I send? And who will go for us?" And I said, "Here am I. Send me!"

I wonder how many of us would've been as willing as Isaiah was to jump straight in and volunteer his service in this way? He does an amazing thing here; he doesn't even know what God is going to ask him to do or where he is going to send him and yet he is ready and willing to go – simply because God needs someone! We could all learn a lot from Isaiah here!

May I encourage you today, to be ready to hear God's voice - just as Isaiah was. You will then be able to hear what God is asking you to do for him. It won't necessarily be a large and daunting task – it may well be something quite simple and straight forward and easy for you to do. You will be amazed at the fulfilment it will bring you!

O Lord, I am amazed at Isaiah's readiness to go for you, and do what you wanted him to do. Please help me to hear your voice when you need me to respond in a similar fashion and for me to be as ready as Isaiah was to be sent! Amen.

11 AUGUST

Ever Ready

Isaiah 21 v 8: … Day after day, my lord, I stand on the watchtower; every night I stay at my post.

As Christian believers we are never off duty and we never retire. We are on-call 24/7, readily available for the call of our Master – who may even wake us in the middle of the night with an urgent desire to pray! There is no time of day or night when we can't offer up prayers to our God; He never sleeps, so is always there to hear us! Similarly we are also available to do whatever else he may ask us to do. This is why the Christian Life can be so exciting; if we allow ourselves to be totally led by the Holy Spirit we never know what's going to happen next!

I think, if we're honest, we all tend to earmark some special time for ourselves, which is perfectly alright as long as we are willing to let go of it should we be asked to – ever ready to respond to our Master's voice.

Thank you Father, my Lord and Master, that you are always there for me 24/7 – please help me to be available for you 24/7 too. Amen.

12 AUGUST

Perfect Peace

Isaiah 26 v 3: You will keep in perfect peace him whose mind is steadfast, because he trusts in you.

I think you will agree with me that 'peace' is one of the most sought after states of mind; after all, who wouldn't prefer to be at peace rather than completely stressed out during a most challenging time? But maybe you think this is impossible?

The great news I have for you today is, that if you can keep your eyes fully on the Lord and can totally trust him with every aspect of your difficult situation – handing it all over to him, as you go through it – amazingly you will find yourself feeling a great sense of peace, a perfect peace, like you have never known before!

Next time you face a challenging time – try it and see!

Thank you Lord God, for giving me this promise of 'peace' as long as I stay focused on You - trusting You with it all. May I remember this whenever I face trials of any kind, whether large or small. Amen.

13 AUGUST

True Worshippers

Isaiah 29 v 13: ... These people come near to me with their mouth and honour me with their lips, but their hearts are far from me. Their worship of me is made up only of rules taught by men.

God isn't fooled for a minute – he looks right into our hearts and sees who the true worshippers are. He can tell when someone is just going through the motions and paying lip service; and let's be honest we've probably all been guilty of doing this at some point. But it is the on-going fake worship that really upsets God, for he longs to be worshipped in Spirit and in Truth!

As we come before our God to worship him, we need to give ourselves a quick heart check, to make sure that we are truly engaging with what we are singing and saying. May we be amongst those who are known as the true worshippers of God!

Please forgive me Lord if I have not been worshipping you in truth, if I have let my mind wander and have not been thinking about what I've been saying. I love you Lord and long to worship you with all that I have and with all that I am. Amen.

14 AUGUST

Running from God?

Isaiah 30 v 15: ... In repentance and rest is your salvation, in quietness and trust is your strength, but you would have none of it.

In this verse, God is showing us how we can benefit in life but we need to be willing to change - to turn away from the wrong things we are doing and to rest in God. The ways of God are not what the world places value on, and so we quite often don't want to know. We want to run our own lives in the way we want to – doing our own thing, not wanting anyone to tell us what to do. And yet it is when we are calm and trusting God that we find our greatest strength – not when we are trying to go it alone, trying to make things happen apart from God.

Your heavenly Father knows exactly what you need and only ever has your best interests at heart. Think of his great sadness when he sees one of his beloved children running away from him, ignoring his words. I wonder today, are you running from God? If so, it's not too late to turn around and come back to Him. Pray with me.

O Heavenly Father, I am so sorry for refusing your wise guidance and for going my own way; I repent right now and choose to rest and trust in You. Amen.

15 AUGUST

Fit for Service?

Isaiah 33 v 23: Your rigging hangs loose: The mast is not held secure, the sail is not spread.

Our verse for today is something of a 'wake up' call, urging us to take a close look at ourselves and find out just how fit we are for Christian service.

The boat described in this verse wouldn't get very far in the condition it is in and I wonder what your loose rigging could be. Maybe your time spent with God has become rather slack? And how about your mast that is no longer secure? Maybe your faith is not as strong as it once was? And how about the sail that isn't spread? Maybe you are not opening yourself up fully to the work and ministry of the Holy Spirit in your life?

I am hoping that, rather than feeling condemned, you will feel encouraged to get ship shape once again and set sail into whatever God has for you out there, on the horizon!

Thank you Lord, for giving me this 'wake up' call today, and for encouraging me to take a closer look at myself. I am sorry for the things I have let slip; please help me to make any adjustments that are needed so that I am fit for Kingdom Service! Amen.

16 AUGUST

His Tender Care

Isaiah 40 v 11: He tends his flock like a shepherd: He gathers the lambs in his arms and carries them close to his heart; he gently leads those that have young.

I just love this analogy of how our Lord looks after us; it shows how mindful he is of the weakest among us by paying them special and close attention. It shows his heart for the youngest and most vulnerable, and his desire to hold us close to his heart.

Instead of seeing our weakness and vulnerability as a bad thing in God's sight, let us look at it as a great opportunity for us to be loved and cared for by Him even more intimately, for that is what He longs to do.

For any parents out there who are struggling today – hold onto His promise to 'gently' lead you! Don't put yourself under all that extra pressure to become the 'perfect parent' – there is no such thing; He will lead you!

Thank you Heavenly Father for your tender love and care; in a sense we are all your lambs and long to be held close to your heart. Whenever I feel weak, help me remember this Lord. Amen.

17 AUGUST

Supernatural Strength

Isaiah 40 v 31: ... but those who hope in the LORD will renew their strength. They will soar on wings like eagles; they will run and not grow weary, they will walk and not be faint.

Weariness can hit any of us at any time. As it says in the preceding verse, 'Even youths grow tired and weary'! But we need not despair when we find ourselves in this situation, because God knows we need energy to continue with our work and he is more than able to give us supernatural strength to enable us to carry on, and to an even greater capacity than we would otherwise have had! But this only comes about if we put our hope in God, or 'wait on the Lord' as some translations of the bible describe it. We need to stop what we are trying to do and take time out to focus on our God, and then He will come through for us.

Next time you find yourself flagging and you still have commitments to fulfil – turn to God for His help and enabling – He won't let you down!

O Lord my God, you are so amazing – thank you that you can renew my strength. Please remind me to take the time to ask for your help. Amen.

18 AUGUST

Holding My Hand

Isaiah 41 v 13: For I am the LORD, your God, who takes hold of your right hand and says to you, Do not fear; I will help you.

When faced with a frightening situation, if we truly believed in this verse then our fear would vanish – just like that! Why is it, I wonder, that we so often forget God's Word in the midst of a crisis?

Let us meditate on this verse together – so that it really sinks in and resides within us. First, He is OUR God, we belong to Him and he is ours! Just stop and think about that for a moment. Secondly, God says that he takes hold of your right hand. Imagine that! The God of the Universe actually holding your right hand! Wow! Thirdly, he tells you and I not to fear, which implies it must be possible not to! If the God of the whole of creation is really and truly holding our right hand then how can we be afraid, with Him right there beside us? And finally, as if all this wasn't enough, He promises to Help us! What we need to do, next time we face a crisis, is to stop and remember all this!

O Lord, may I meditate on, and trust in this word for me today and draw on it whenever the need arises. Amen.

19 AUGUST

Doing a New Thing

Isaiah 42 v 9: See, the former things have taken place, and new things I declare; before they spring into being I announce them to you.

God is always moving and doing something new and we need to be aware of this fact. He doesn't want us to be doing the same old thing all the time. What may have worked and been right at one time may no longer be working or right for us now. If God closes one door you can be sure that, in His perfect timing, He will open another!

I strongly believe this verse is a prophetic word for someone, if not for several people, today. This is the confirmation you have been waiting for - that God has now finished with what you have been doing and has new things lined up for you on the horizon.

Thank you Lord; you are a God who is always on the move and you like to do new things in and through us. May we be fully open to your guidance in our lives; may we know when you are finished with us in one area and want to move us on to something new. Amen.

20 AUGUST

With You

Isaiah 43 v 2: When you pass through the waters, I will be with you; and when you pass through the rivers, they will not sweep over you. When you walk through the fire, you will not be burned; the flames will not set you ablaze.

When facing storms in this life, God never promises to take us out of them, although he may sometimes do this; but he does promise us two things. First, that He will be with us through the storm and secondly, the storm won't be the end of us.

When on your own in a frightening situation it can be easy to forget God's promises, but if we really believe Him, and we choose to trust Him, we will sense His presence there with us and discover that we are not alone as we thought. He really is there with us, helping us to get through it all. God will not let the storm destroy us or take us away from him. He will carry us through it, giving us all we need to deal with it every step of the way!

Dear Lord, my God, thank you for your promise to be with me through every difficulty I go through. Next time I find myself in deep waters or going through a fire in life, may I cling on to the fact that I am not alone in this situation, but I have You right there with me! Amen.

21 AUGUST

He Prepares the Way

Isaiah 45 v 2: I will go before you and will level the mountains; I will break down gates of bronze and cut through bars of iron.

So often we embark on a course and find we come up against numerous difficulties, but did we pray before we began and asked God to go before us and prepare the way? May I encourage you, if you don't already do this, to try it!

I wonder today, are you facing insurmountable obstacles on your life's journey? Well it's not too late to ask God to go before you and deal with them for you. If what you are doing is in His will then he will break down all those barriers that are standing in the way of your ultimate goal. God has it covered; he sees what's up ahead long before you do! Isn't this great news; it takes all the worry away as you Trust God with it all? This word is for you today!

O Heavenly Father, what comfort and peace your word brings to me today. To know that You are going ahead of me to prepare the way is just amazing – thank you Lord! Please remind me to submit everything to you in prayer before I venture out next time. Amen.

22 AUGUST

He Took My Place

Isaiah 53 v 5: But he was pierced for our transgressions, he was crushed for our iniquities; the punishment that brought us peace was upon him, and by his wounds we are healed.

This verse is worth reading and re-reading until the words fully sink in. From Jesus's suffering and pain we are the ones who gain. For all our wrongdoing he gives us 'peace' and for our sicknesses he brings us 'healing'; this all made possible by his terrible suffering and torturous death on a cross. How can this be? I deserved to be where Jesus was and yet he gladly took my place. He was wounded for my healing and He died to give me "peace".

I am conscious that there may be someone reading this today who's never fully understood what Jesus did on the cross, and today you've seen it – it all makes sense! Jesus was sent by God and willingly gave his life for you - so you could be at peace with God and know him as your Father.

Thank you God for opening my eyes to what Jesus has done for me on the cross; I accept that he has paid the price for me. I turn away from all I know to be wrong and I want to know you as my Father and Jesus as my friend – come into my life I pray. Amen.

23 AUGUST

Higher Ways

Isaiah 55 v 9: As the heavens are higher than the earth, so are my ways higher than your ways and my thoughts than your thoughts.

While living here on earth, we only see things from a very limited perspective. We cannot see everything as God does and therefore we can easily make wrong plans, choices or decisions for both ourselves and others. But God is far above us; he knows exactly what needs to be done and when and why.

Next time you find yourself questioning God or just not understanding what is going on in your life – always remember that God sees the bigger picture. Just for a moment, imagine your life as a 'tapestry' – God is looking down on it and sees how beautiful it all looks, whereas from your position, underneath it, all you can see is a big tangled mess! It is all about perspective. With God's perspective on life, everything makes sense and fits into place just perfectly. He knows what he's doing!

Dear Lord, next time I am wondering what is going on, help me to remember that in heaven, all things are being worked into your perfect plan for my life. For your thoughts and your ways are far above mine! Amen.

24 AUGUST

Answered Prayers

Isaiah 65 v 24: Before they call I will answer; while they are still speaking I will hear.

What an amazing God we have. He already knows what's on our hearts, he knows what we are going to pray about before we even open our mouths, and as it says in today's verse – he will answer us before we've spoken a word! Wow, if we really believed this, it would instantly transform our prayer life!

If we are honest, we often find ourselves unsure of God's interest in our seemingly trivial prayer needs and can't imagine he has the time to want to answer them with so much else going on in the world, so we tend to doubt that he will answer our heart's cry; we feel so unworthy. But the complete opposite is true – He is very much interested in the cry of His child and he cannot wait to hear your voice and to meet your needs! Now doesn't that motivate you to pray more?

I can hardly believe it Lord, that you are already answering my prayer; yes this actual prayer! Thank you! Stir me up to want to pray more; help me enjoy it and look forward to it, just as you do Lord. Amen.

25 AUGUST
Wrong Sources

Jeremiah 2 v 18: Now why go to Egypt to drink water from the Shihor? And why go to Assyria to drink water from the River?

Can you hear the cry of God's heart here? He can see his beloved people going to other sources of sustenance, which he knows are not good for them, instead of coming to Him! He is saying here that He is their life-giving water – he has everything they need; they don't need to go looking elsewhere!

I wonder today, are we tempted to turn aside to the wrong sources for our inner well-being? When seeking guidance do we turn to our horoscope or a palm reader? When seeking comfort do we watch movies and eat popcorn? When feeling lonely do we seek satisfaction in all the wrong places?

Come to the Lord and drink deeply of His love. That is His hearts cry and invitation to you today!

O Father, it's so tempting to look for satisfaction elsewhere. Please forgive me for doing this; cause me to remember that you have everything I need and more! May I come and drink from the river of your delight. Amen.

26 AUGUST

Which Way?

Jeremiah 6 v 16: ... Stand at the crossroads and look; ask for the ancient paths, ask where the good way is, and walk in it, and you will find rest for your souls.

We sometimes come to those landmark moments in our lives where we need to stop and take stock and then decide which direction to proceed in. In today's verse we are advised to ask for the old ways. Not that there is anything wrong with new ways of doing things, but we don't want to ignore the wisdom of those who have gone before us, who have 'walked the walk' so to speak and have learnt what works and what doesn't. They have learnt how to walk in the right way – the tried and tested way - the good way that leads to rest for our souls!

If you happen to be at a crossroads in your life right now, then maybe it would be good to seek some wise counsel? Find someone who's been a Christian for a while and who knows God's Word inside out; ask what they would recommend.

Thank you for today's reminder Lord, that we need to hold the old ways of doing things as dear and to appreciate all the good things the older generations have to offer us. Amen.

27 AUGUST

Taste and See

Jeremiah 15 v 16: When your words came, I ate them; they were my joy and my heart's delight, for I bear your name, O LORD God Almighty.

When God speaks directly to us and into our situation, the moment is almost beyond words; that amazing sense of the Lord wanting to speak to me personally is just incredible! His words penetrate our inner being and we sense that joy bubbling up within us!

God's word is sharp and active, getting right to the point of what's troubling us, or giving us that word of encouragement we so desperately need. Receiving His word is very similar to the delight of consuming our favourite meal. You can feel it sustaining and strengthening you, leaving you feeling satisfied and comforted inside.

I hope this encourages you to want to hear from God more often, either through reading His word or sensing what he is saying to you through other means. We are his children and we need to hear our Father's voice!

O Father, thank you for your 'word' to me today. It has stirred up a yearning in my heart to hear more from you; thank you that you want to talk to me - your child. Amen.

28 AUGUST

Rooted in God

Jeremiah 17 v 8: He will be like a tree planted by the water that sends out its roots by the stream. It does not fear when heat comes; its leaves are always green. It has no worries in a year of drought and never fails to bear fruit.

Who will become like this tree? Answer – anyone who puts their full trust and confidence in God! This sounds very simple and in effect it is – but we need to reach that place, like the tree, where we are fully relying on God for our nourishment, strength and growth. In other words, we need to plant our roots in God alone!

Just like the tree whose roots have gone deep into the soil to find moisture, we need to go deeper into the things of the Lord to receive our food, then we, like the tree, will not be afraid when trouble comes our way – we will remain stable and strong and able to help others in their distress. No longer will we worry, because we will have that assurance deep down, that God is there for us and will provide all we need – such a blessed place to be!

Please forgive me Lord for not fully trusting you, my roots are so often reaching out to other things. Thank you for showing me how I can live a worry-free life. Amen.

29 AUGUST

Putty in His Hands

Jeremiah 18 v 4: But the pot he was shaping from the clay was marred in his hands; so the potter formed it into another pot, shaping it as seemed best to him.

Ever felt in a complete mess? You don't seem to be fulfilling the purpose you thought you were made for? You feel you've lost your way in God? Then take heart from our verse for today and see what the potter can do with the clay! God is the potter and we are the clay; he can make us into whatever he wants us to be – as seems best to him! God can transform you! Come to him humbly, recognising your need of the potter's hands. Give up trying to re-shape yourself and instead hand yourself and your life completely over to Him – letting him have His way!

There's nothing so bad you can do to cause the potter to throw you away; he will always be there waiting to transform you. All you need to do is ask Him and become putty in His hands!

How can I thank you enough Lord, for never giving up on me, even when I have made a mess of things. I give myself into your hands and ask you to re-make me. Amen.

30 AUGUST

Can't Keep It In!

Jeremiah 20 v 9: But if I say, "I will not mention him or speak any more in his name," his word is in my heart like a fire, a fire shut up in my bones. I am weary of holding it in; indeed, I cannot.

Imagine being so full of God's word that it feels like a fire burning inside you, so strong that you can't keep it in any longer. How different our lives would be if we felt like Jeremiah and couldn't keep God's word inside us, but had to let it out by sharing it with others; think how many people would be blessed! In view of this, perhaps it would be a good idea to pray and ask God to cause His word to burn within us, so much so that it starts bursting out, almost without us knowing, as we begin to automatically share it as part of our everyday conversation. I don't mean quoting chapter and verse, but that God's word will naturally affect our views, opinions and attitudes as we speak to people, so that as a result, we are sharing with them how God sees things.

Please Lord God, burn your word deep into my heart as I read it, so that such a fire is stirred within me, that I cannot help but release it into the world! Amen.

31 AUGUST

Beware of False Prophets

Jeremiah 23 v 21: I did not send these prophets, yet they have run with their message; I did not speak to them, yet they have prophesied.

Along with the genuine prophets of God who speak God's Word correctly, are those who don't, and sometimes it can be very hard to tell the difference.

We are told to test things - to check that what we hear from preachers and teachers agrees with the scriptures. Not everyone that says, 'The Lord told me', or 'The Lord says' has actually been told anything by the Lord and we would be wise to remember this and not just take on board what anyone with an upfront ministry tells us. We need to take it to the Lord in prayer, especially if we feel in any way uncomfortable in our spirit or start to lose our sense of 'peace'. For just as in Jeremiah's time, many false prophets are amongst us right now!

Thank you Father, for bringing this to my attention today, I can see how important it is to check things out with You whenever I am unsure. Please make me extra sensitive to those inner nudges of discomfort that come from your Holy Spirit when something isn't really coming from you, and help me warn others too. Amen.

01 SEPTEMBER

Hope for the Future

Jeremiah 29 v 11: "For I know the plans I have for you,"
declares the LORD, "plans to prosper you and not to harm
you, plans to give you hope and a future."

This verse is such a powerful one because of the 'hope' it brings, and it is such a good verse to share with others when they are going through a particularly rough time.

It's something we all need - 'hope', and not the kind of vague hope the world gives us that things will get better soon. No, the 'hope' we are talking about here is a 'hope' that is certain. We know things are definitely going to improve because God has said so and we believe in Him who holds our future! This remains true even if things go wrong in our lives because we trust that our God will be using every moment to bring about good in our lives, and in the lives of those around us. This is True Hope, for we know that God only wants what is ultimately good for us!

Thank you Lord, that you have good plans for my future. Even
if I have to pass through difficulties along the way I still have
'hope' as everything is in Your hands. Amen.

02 SEPTEMBER

Times of Refreshing

Jeremiah 31 v 25: I will refresh the weary and satisfy the faint.

Do you have times of feeling weary and faint? Maybe that's exactly how you are feeling today, and if so: this word has come at just the right time! God is so good, he knows exactly what you need to hear and when.

God has promised to refresh us whenever we are tired or worn out and feel we can no longer function properly, but we need to choose to receive that promise by faith. We need to focus on God instead of our weariness and strengthen ourselves in Him. As we draw close to God he will sustain us with all we need to continue, and not only that, he will 'refresh' our souls from deep within. Doesn't that sound wonderful – just the word 'refresh' itself makes you feel fresher and brighter inside! We need to come to be 'refreshed' on a regular basis, even when we don't feel particularly weary.

O Lord, you know how some days are a real struggle to get through; it's like someone has turned off my energy supply. Thank you for encouraging me today. I come now and receive your promise, I receive your inner refreshing, I receive your life-giving infusion. Amen.

03 SEPTEMBER

Nothing is Too Hard

Jeremiah 32 v 17: Ah, Sovereign LORD, you have made the heavens and the earth by your great power and outstretched arm. Nothing is too hard for you.

Whenever doubts start crowding in - that God won't come through for you in this situation - take time out to consider today's verse. Think about it. If our God made everything that we can see, and even those things we can't, is anything too hard for Him?

The truth is - Nothing is impossible with God - absolutely Nothing! Sometimes he may not act as soon as we would like him to and sometimes the answer may be 'no' or 'not yet', but he is always more than able to do it! Even the biggest tangle we get ourselves into he is able to unravel! If you make a mistake, if you go the wrong way, if you make the wrong decision - God is always more than able to get you back to where you should be – on the right track!

O what a comfort that is Father, to know that whatever mess I find myself in, You are more than able to put things right, for nothing is too hard for you. Amen.

04 SEPTEMBER

Promise of Restoration

Jeremiah 33 v 7: I will bring Judah and Israel back from captivity and will rebuild them as they were before.

The nations of Judah and Israel had both rebelled greatly against the Lord their God, by worshipping other gods and by refusing to follow him or listen to his commands. As a result, they were taken captive into Babylon; but God hadn't forgotten them. He still loved His people and had a plan to bring about their complete restoration.

Whenever God disciplines us, it is always for our ultimate good. If we rebel and refuse to listen to his warnings, we will face the consequences of our actions, but God is always ready, willing and able to restore our broken relationship with Him.

If you are reading this today feeling very far from God –then know this right now – God sees you, he loves you and he longs to restore you back into the person you were always meant to be – his lovely and precious child.

O loving Father, can this really be true? Please forgive me for all my rebellious ways and bring me back to You. I just want things to be back as they used to be between us. I love you and long to serve you. Amen.

05 SEPTEMBER

God's Indestructible Word

Jeremiah 36 v 28: Take another scroll and write on it all the words that were on the first scroll, which Jehoiakim king of Judah burned up.

This is what happened when Jeremiah was given a message for the people of Judah and told to write it on a scroll. As the king heard it being read, he cut off strips, one at a time, and threw them into the fire until the whole scroll was consumed! But Jeremiah is then told, by the Lord, to re-write the words on a fresh scroll. You cannot snuff out God's Word; he will have His say, no matter what!

Have you ever noticed that when God wants to tell us something and we don't get it the first time around or we don't really listen or take it as seriously as we should, he will always find a way to bring back that very same message to us? Nothing can hinder God from speaking - when he wants to tell us something important he will, and no one can stop you from hearing him. What a blessing this is!

Thank you Lord, that nothing can destroy your Word; when you speak to me, may I listen! Amen.

06 SEPTEMBER

Do Not Fear

Jeremiah 42 v 11: Do not be afraid of the king of Babylon, whom you now fear. Do not be afraid of him, declares the LORD, for I am with you and will save you and deliver you from his hands.

I wonder, do you have a 'king of Babylon' in your life - someone you are afraid of right now? Or it could be something you are afraid of? Or maybe you get really afraid of the devil and all his evil works? If you re-read today's verse, replacing 'the king of Babylon' with whatever or whoever you're afraid of – it will speak in a very powerful and personal way to you, if it hasn't done so already. Try it now!

I am hoping that the power of God's word has brought you a measure of 'peace' today and that you can feel secure, knowing that God has your back. He has everything under control. No weapon formed against you shall prosper. You are safe in His arms.

Thank you Lord for your words of comfort and reassurance to me today; help me look to You whenever I feel afraid and to trust that you will always be there for me. Amen.

07 SEPTEMBER

Tough Love

Lamentations 3 v 32: Though he brings grief, he will show compassion, so great is his unfailing love.

You may well have heard it said that God will never bring us any grief, but what loving and caring parent would never discipline their child? When we look at today's verse in this context, we can see why God may sometimes cause us pain in order to teach and train us in what is right and wrong, and to show us where we should be heading. Please realise that this is God's tough love for us and it is always for our ultimate good!

Just as a parent will often struggle watching their child suffer as a result of their discipline, so too does God, and he longs to comfort us as soon as the grief is over.

Thank you Lord, that you love me too much to leave me just as I am. Please help me recognise when you are trying to teach me something and help me respond. I know you only want what is best for me and that any grief you may bring into my life springs from a heart of love – a love that never fails.
Amen.

08 SEPTEMBER

Led by the Spirit

Ezekiel 1 v 12: Each one went straight ahead. Wherever the spirit would go, they would go, without turning as they went.

Oh, what a wonderful description of how to live a Spirit-led life; one in which we follow God's every move! We keep our focus directly on where He takes us; we move straight ahead, without turning. In other words, we let nothing distract us or draw us away from the Spirit's leading. Oh to be able to live just like the four living creatures that Ezekiel describes so vividly - if only!

How much better our lives would be if we lived in this way; only going where God wants us to go, only doing the things God wants us to do, and not allowing ourselves to be led away from His perfect path for us. Don't you just long to live this way? Why not ask God to show you how? If today's word has really touched your heart, then pray this prayer with true conviction.

O Lord God, something has been stirred deep within me today, and I now have a longing to follow you even closer than ever. Please show me and teach me how I can be fully led by your Spirit; I look forward to where you are going to take me. Amen.

09 SEPTEMBER

Idolatry in God's House

Ezekiel 8 v 12: He said to me, "Son of man, have you seen what the elders of the house of Israel are doing in the darkness, each at the shrine of his own idol? They say, 'The LORD does not see us; the LORD has forsaken the land.'"

Idolatry today is just as much a problem as it was back in Ezekiel's time. It may not be as obvious as it was back then (which is why they attempted to hide it under the cover of darkness), but sadly it is often still very present within God's House.

Within the Church, we are still very much in danger of having idols. Worship leaders, preachers, bible teachers, and evangelists can all rise to prominence and be worshipped. Similarly, the people in these positions can easily become puffed up with pride and have their eyes fixed on their 'Ministry' rather than on Jesus. Guard yourself from idols.

Heavenly Father, idolatry breaks your heart - please forgive us! Please forgive me if I have made anything or anyone within your Church an idol. Please highlight anywhere that this may be occurring and give me the grace to confess it to you and turn away from it, in Jesus' name. Amen.

10 SEPTEMBER

God's Spirit Within

Ezekiel 10 v 17: When the cherubim stood still, they also stood still; and when the cherubim rose, they rose with them, because the spirit of the living creatures was in them.

Once again we are reminded that if we have God's Spirit living within us, we will do what he does, when he does. Have you ever had that experience where you hear the same 'message' within a short space of time coming from several different places? The reason this occurs is not only to underline what God wants to say to you, but is also a sign that God's Spirit is very much alive and active amongst his followers They all have one Spirit - God's Spirit - so they all have the same message!

May I ask you some very personal questions today? Do you sense God's Spirit living within you? How important is He in your life? Do you sense Him leading and guiding you through the various events of your everyday life? Challenging questions, I know, but nevertheless well worth asking because this is the life that Jesus died to give you – one in which you become full of God's Spirit!

O Lord, please fill me afresh today with your Holy Spirit
Come inside me and live through me, I pray. Amen.

11 SEPTEMBER

A New Heart

Ezekiel 11 v 19: I will give them an undivided heart and put a new spirit in them; I will remove from them their heart of stone and give them a heart of flesh.

This is one of the most amazing promises in the Old Testament – God is going to deal with the hardness of heart that has plagued the Israelites for pretty much all of their lives.

While they have a heart of stone they cannot respond to God in the way he desires. He wants a close, intimate and loving relationship with them, in which they trust him and are faithful to him, but they will need much softer hearts if this is to become a reality, and the same is true for us!

O for a heart of 'flesh', whereby we can feel and respond to the love God has for us and feel and respond to the needs of those around us.

Thank you Lord that you have provided the way for us to have a new, softer heart. Ezekiel only saw it in the future, but we have it available to us now, since you have given us your Holy Spirit. Soften my heart O God! Amen.

12 SEPTEMBER

God's Heart for the Wicked

Ezekiel 18 v 23: Do I take any pleasure in the death of the wicked? declares the Sovereign LORD. Rather, am I not pleased when they turn from their ways and live?

So many people have completely the wrong view of God; they see him as a cross and angry God who is just waiting to pounce on them for the smallest thing they do wrong. But he loves all mankind, just as a parent loves all of their children, however badly they behave.

Rather than waiting for us to do wrong, as today's verse tells us, God is longing for us to do right - just as a loving parent doesn't want their child to be disobedient, but longs for them to behave well. God is not pleased to see us mess up our lives and he doesn't want us to stay that way. Just as a good parent will discipline their child for their own good, so also will a good and loving God. He loves us far too much to leave us as we are and he is thrilled when anyone turns from their ways and lives!

Thank you so much Father for showing me your true heart towards all mankind; and that includes me. Whenever I choose to go astray from your word, I now know that you long for me to turn from my ways back to yours. Please help me to love others - just as you do. Amen.

13 SEPTEMBER

Keep Sunday Special

Ezekiel 20 v 20: Keep my Sabbaths holy, that they may be a sign between us. Then you will know that I am the LORD your God.

The amazing 'treasure' hidden within this verse can be easily overlooked at first glance. Not only is our Lord commanding us to keep His Sabbaths holy, but he is also drawing our attention to the 'special' relationship we have with Him. He speaks of the Sabbaths being a sign between us and keeping them, shows the world we belong to Him and take Him seriously. Our obedience causes us to be that much closer to our God and aware of who He is!

If God rested after His work, then we certainly need to rest after ours! Our Lord knows that we need to have times of rest for our physical, spiritual and emotional well-being; but so many of us ignore this profound wisdom, sadly, at our own peril. Our constant busyness is one of the reasons we have so many mental and physical health issues today.

Change my heart O Lord; may I strongly desire to keep Sundays special, as it is a day you have given us as a gift – for us to both rest and to draw close to you. Amen.

14 SEPTEMBER

False Gods, False Hope

Ezekiel 29 v 16: Egypt will no longer be a source of confidence for the people of Israel but will be a reminder of their sin in turning to her for help. Then they will know that I am the Sovereign LORD.

Who or what do you turn to in troubled times? Maybe it's to your family or your friends? Maybe it's to food or drink or to something else that you really enjoy doing? The problem with all of these props is that they will all let you down! Props, by their very nature, can always be knocked right out from beneath you and when they are, you realise that it was God you should have turned to all along. He alone is your help and support in difficult times because he will never fail you or let you down.

So next time you face a crisis, or you need help with something - try turning to God! He may well send someone your way to comfort you or help out with any practicalities - but always turn to him first!

Please forgive me Lord for relying on other people or things to get me through a tough patch; please remind me next time to cry out to You! Amen.

15 SEPTEMBER

The Hope of Repentance

Ezekiel 33 v 19: And if a wicked man turns away from his wickedness and does what is just and right, he will live by doing so.

Without hope, a man's heart grows sick within him, for we all need hope and today's verse gives us all 'hope' – the hope of Repentance!

When it comes to God's forgiveness, we are all on a level playing field. God grants us all the opportunity to turn from our sinful ways and turn to Him - the giver of Eternal Life - by doing what is good, right, true and just. But sin seems to be an out of date concept these days - surely this can't have any relevance for us can it? Whether we believe it or not we all still have need of a Saviour and sometimes we need Him to save us from ourselves! If they had this hope in Ezekiel's time, how much more do we have it now? No matter what you have done wrong, there is always a way back to God – simply turn away from the wrong and do right.

O Father God you are so good. Your heart is ever waiting for the sinner to return to You, just as a Father waits for his lost son - so eager to forgive him and pour his blessings on him. Why would I ever want to stray again? Amen.

16 SEPTEMBER

Good Shepherd

Ezekiel 34 v 12: As a shepherd looks after his scattered flock when he is with them, so will I look after my sheep. I will rescue them from all the places where they were scattered on a day of clouds and darkness.

Next time you are having a bad day and everything thing feels black and heavy, and you have lost your joy and feel far from your Saviour – remember that it is then, as your Good Shepherd, that God searches for you, making every effort to find you and not content until he can pick you up in his arms and carry you home on his shoulders, bringing you back into the safety of His Fold and rejoicing that he has found his lost sheep!

I have a very strong impression that these words are speaking directly to someone today – let your shepherd come and find you!

O Lord, how I need you. Thank you that you come searching for me whenever I am lost, afraid or hurting. I have no energy left to put up a fight, so I gladly submit myself into the care and loving arms of my Good Shepherd. Amen.

17 SEPTEMBER

Revival

Ezekiel 37 v 3: He asked me, "Son of man, can these bones live?" I said, "O Sovereign LORD, you alone know."

Appearances do not bother our Lord. However dead something might seem to us – in God's eyes it can always be brought back to life! In this amazing account of the dry bones coming alive, it is well worth reading the whole passage, we see how God asks Ezekiel to speak to the bones and stage by stage they develop, until they rise up to become a mighty army for God.

Are your spirits flagging? Does everything around you seem dead? Why not try doing what Ezekiel did and speak positive words into these hopeless looking situations – speak life into them rather than death and stand back and see what your God can do? He can see the full potential in any given set of circumstances, so why not choose to believe the positive rather than what your eyes are telling you?

Nothing is impossible with you Lord. Thank you that you can breathe new life into anything or anyone; please breathe new life into me today, for your glory. Amen.

18 SEPTEMBER

The Inner Sanctuary

Ezekiel 43 v 5: Then the Spirit lifted me up and brought me into the inner court, and the glory of the LORD filled the temple.

It is interesting to me that as Ezekiel is brought into the 'inner court', the Lord's glory fills the temple. There is a message here for us I believe. When we take ourselves off, and find a quiet inner place of peace, calm and safety in the Lord, we will then, in the stillness, sense His glory filling our entire being, making us acutely aware of his presence, so that we can receive from him anything he chooses to reveal to us. Such times as this are sheer bliss; a taste of heaven here on earth.

Today, in our increasingly busy world, how much more do we need to enter that inner sanctuary - that place of peace and safety, where we experience God's glory, in such a special and intimate way.

O Father, how I long to come into your inner courts to see Your glory, and to be filled with You to overflowing. Thank you for the inner sanctuary, where we can come and truly worship you. Amen.

19 SEPTEMBER
Let It Flow

Ezekiel 47 v 8: ... This water flows towards the eastern region and goes down into the Arabah, where it enters the Sea. When it empties into the Sea, the water there becomes fresh.

Today's verse is a wonderful illustration of how God's Spirit flows out, like a river, from God's presence and heals everything in its path – even the salty sea water is made 'fresh' in its wake!

I wonder, do you have any 'salty' areas in your life right now; areas that need the touch of God's Life Giving Spirit? Why not open yourself up, like the Sea, to receive this healing water that flows out from God's temple - bringing Life to everything it touches. Allow God's Spirit to flow into those barren areas of your life and bring a freshness and newness that you never dreamed of. God is in the business of transformations.

O Lord, here I am, standing before you like an ocean, deep and wide – ready to receive your Life Giving water. I invite your Holy Spirit to flow into me and overwhelm every part - making all things fresh and new. Amen.

20 SEPTEMBER

Night Vision

Daniel 2 v 19: During the night the mystery was revealed to Daniel in a vision. Then Daniel praised the God of heaven...

Never rule out God speaking to you during the night, either in a vision or a dream. In fact, this is probably one of the easiest ways for us to be able to hear from God, when we are still and truly rested without any distractions!

Daniel needed God to show him the meaning of King Nebuchadnezzar's dream - his very life depended upon it! Sometimes, you too might desperately need to hear God's solution regarding a situation you are in. I wonder, are you in such a situation now? Then cry out to God and ask him to speak to you - yes, even in the night! May God answer your cry and clearly show you what you so desperately need to know. If you don't have a current problem, it's always a good idea to commit yourself to God each night before you sleep and ask him to guide and protect your dreams.

Thank you Lord. You came to Daniel's aid during the night by revealing the meaning of the king's dream. O Lord, I am more than ready for you to speak to me during the night; please help me remember to commit my sleeping hours to you each night. Amen.

21 SEPTEMBER

Even If He Does Not

Daniel 3 v 18: But even if he does not, we want you to know, O king, that we will not serve your gods or worship the image of gold you have set up.

Have you ever been forced to decide between following God or doing something else? Well if you have, you will know something of the dilemma facing Daniel's three friends in today's verse – because if they didn't bow down and worship the king's statue they would be thrown into a fiery furnace! Hopefully, your situation wasn't that drastic!

What is so amazing here is that the three friends are quite willing to die for their faith and under no circumstances will they give in and worship any other god. Yes, even if God doesn't save them, they are still quite willing to place their lives into God's hands and allow him to decide their fate! Have you ever done that? Shadrach, Meshach and Abednego believed in God's sovereignty; they knew he had the final say over what would happen to them and they were content to rest in and trust in their God. O that we would all have faith and trust like theirs!

I come, humbled, my Lord. These three men have taught me so much today; please help me to utterly abandon myself to your ultimate plan for my life. Amen.

22 SEPTEMBER

Living Witness

Daniel 6 v 20: When he came near the den, he called to Daniel in an anguished voice, "Daniel, servant of the living God, has your God, whom you serve continually, been able to rescue you from the lions?"

You never know who is watching and noticing the way you live, or how your life might be influencing theirs - well not until it is forced out into the open by circumstances!

King Darius was tricked into issuing a decree which, in turn, sadly led to Daniel being thrown to the lions! Darius was so distraught over this outcome that he hadn't eaten or slept all night and now he calls out to Daniel in the desperate hope that his God has saved him. King Darius had seen Daniel's faith in action and it had made an impression on him. He knew he had continued to pray three times a day despite the threat of the lions.

When Darius saw that God had indeed rescued Daniel he ordered that everyone should fear and revere the God of Daniel. So, you never know what influence you might be having!

May I be as faithful to you as Daniel was Lord and may I continue to be a witness for you as long as I live. Amen.

23 SEPTEMBER

God's Strength

Daniel 10 v 19: "Do not be afraid, O man highly esteemed," he said. "Peace! Be strong now; be strong." When he spoke to me, I was strengthened and said, "Speak, my lord, since you have given me strength."

Are you feeling weak today? Lacking in energy and motivation? Feeling unprepared and ill-equipped for what lays ahead? Then re-read these words today and hear them being spoken to you and by you.

It is so lovely to hear the voice of the Lord, especially when he has such comforting and encouraging words to speak to us. Daniel was strengthened while he was still being spoken to, and he was fully aware that the strength he now had wasn't his own, but was God's strength!

Daniel needed this strength to be able to cope with the awesome message he was about to receive. Are you facing something rather daunting right now? Then ask God to strengthen you with His mighty strength!

Thank you Lord, for your encouraging words to me today; thank you for reminding me that my strength comes from You. Please forgive me for the times I still try to rely on my own. Amen.

24 SEPTEMBER

Door of Hope

Hosea 2 v 15: There I will give her back her vineyards, and will make the valley of Achor a door of hope.

Have you ever felt as though you were in a deep, dark valley of trouble, with no way out? Maybe you feel like that now? The word 'Achor' means trouble, and in today's verse God is promising to turn things around for Israel, by changing their terrible situation into a door of hope!

Israel had turned away from God, choosing to worship idols instead, and had consequently paid the price by losing everything they held dear. But now God is promising to restore things to them and he is making a way for them to escape from their valley experience. In fact, he even promises to use these very experiences to create a doorway of hope! And that is exactly what he is saying to you today!

I thank you Father that you see me in the valleys and that you long to use these experiences to build up my character and to help others, as I share with them what I have learnt whilst in the valley - the valley becomes a door of hope instead of just a time of trouble. Amen.

25 SEPTEMBER

He Will Come to Us

Hosea 6 v 3: Let us acknowledge the LORD; let us press on to acknowledge him. As surely as the sun rises, he will appear; he will come to us like the winter rains, like the spring rains that water the earth.

There are several places in God's word where he promises to come and meet with us if we will make the effort to find him, come close to him and revere him for who he really is. Why would we not want to do this? Especially when he is described as coming like rain!

Rain is something we all desperately need, without it we would die; if this is true in the natural, how much more is it true in the spiritual? In other words, we desperately need our God to come to us like the rain because we all need his presence, to give us real spiritual life in order for us to thrive. And so today, let us press on and acknowledge our God for who he is and wait for him to come to us. Let us set aside time to do this on a regular basis that we may be nourished by Him.

O Lord I come to you now; I sit at your feet, acknowledging who you are, and I wait... I wait patiently for you to come! Amen.

26 SEPTEMBER

Tainted Worship

Hosea 8 v 11: Though Ephraim built many altars for sin offerings, these have become altars for sinning.

Could this be possible today? Could we inadvertently be worshipping idols instead of the Lord as we carry out our acts of worship to God? 'Surely not', do I hear you say? Yes, it may seem ridiculous to even think such a thought, but I fear at times we are no different to Ephraim, but we just don't see it because it is so subtle!

Could it be that our church and going to our church becomes the most important thing in our life, even overshadowing our commitment to our family at times? We may think we are putting God first, but we are in fact putting 'church' first. Similarly, 'good deeds' can become our source of self-worth – but shouldn't God be in that place? And then there is sung worship – could it be possible to be worshipping the song itself or the worship leader or the joy of music, rather than our Lord? I leave these thoughts with you to ponder…

O Lord forgive us all; thank you for opening my eyes to these pitfalls in worship today and help me to stay out of them in the future; in Jesus' name I ask this. Amen.

27 SEPTEMBER

You Are So Loved

Hosea 11 v 4: I led them with cords of human kindness, with ties of love; I lifted the yoke from their neck and bent down to feed them.

How did this verse make you feel as you read it? Cared for? Loved? Relieved? Secure? Protected? Nurtured? I think a mixture of all these feelings can arise from this verse and I think it is worth us meditating on it for a moment now.

What would happen, I wonder, if you read this at the start of each day and really believed it to be true for you? I think knowing just how much you are loved by God would transform your everyday life. I believe you would be set free from your bondage to fear and be filled with inexpressible joy! But don't take my word for it – I challenge you to try it, and see for yourself!

Thank you Lord for loving me in such a wonderful way. Please take this heavy yoke off my neck; I have been carrying it for far too long now. Thank you for feeding me with your Word today; I have had quite a banquet! Amen.

28 SEPTEMBER

He's for Everyone!

Joel 2 v 28: ... I will pour out my Spirit on all people. Your sons and daughters will prophesy, your old men will dream dreams, your young men will see visions.

Joel speaks here of a time yet to come, but to us who are reading his words now – this time has already come and will continue to come in the future!

In Joel's day, God's Spirit would come upon an individual for a specific task and would sometimes leave again. King David was afraid of this happening to him after he had committed adultery with Bathsheba (see Psalm 51v11). But this new promise, of which Joel is speaking here, was that the Holy Spirit would come upon everyone who believed and would live inside them permanently, giving supernatural gifts to all - making no distinctions between gender or age!

God's Holy Spirit is a person and He longs to come and fill you today. If you believe and trust in Jesus Christ as your Saviour, you need to turn away from all that you know to be wrong and ask for the Holy Spirit to come and fill you – and He will! He is for 'everyone' who truly repents and believes in Jesus.

Come Holy Spirit – Come! Amen.

29 SEPTEMBER

Ready for His Call?

Amos 7 v 15: But the LORD took me from tending the flock and said to me, "Go, prophesy to my people Israel."

What a change for Amos. After being a shepherd and a voice for his sheep he is now called to be God's voice to Israel; I wonder if he found any similarities between the two jobs? Did being a shepherd help prepare him for this new calling? Did the sheep always follow his voice? Will the people of Israel follow his voice?

It may well be that God will call you out from one thing and into another and the first calling may well help you in your next – but are you ready to be called out into something new? Is God asking you to change your job or your ministry, or your whole way of life for him? Maybe today's word is the confirmation you have been waiting for? Or maybe God is just reminding you that he may well have something new for you to do in the future? Either way, we need to stay open to God's direction in our lives, just as Amos did!

Please lead and guide me Lord into whatever calling you have for me up ahead; may I be open to the possibility of change in my life and trust you with it. Amen.

30 SEPTEMBER

Starved of God's Word

Amos 8 v 11: "The days are coming," declares the Sovereign LORD, "when I will send a famine through the land – not a famine of food or a thirst for water, but a famine of hearing the words of the LORD."

This is hard to imagine, I know, but what if we had no access at all to God's Word; what if God no longer spoke to us, no longer guided us or convicted us of our sin. What kind of sorry state would we end up in? With no scriptures to encourage us, no words to speak out against the enemy, what would become of us?

It is so true that you often don't appreciate what you have until it is taken away from you! I am writing this while still in the middle of the Covid-19 pandemic, and have we not all come to realise what is really important to us? Those things and people that we took for granted before are now shown for how special they are to us! So imagine you can no longer hear God's Word – doesn't it make you appreciate what we have?

Forgive us Father, whenever we take your words for granted. Please give me a hunger for your Word – both your words to me personally as well as those contained within the scriptures; I thank you for them! Amen.

01 OCTOBER

The Repair Shop

Amos 9 v 11: In that day I will restore David's fallen tent. I will repair its broken places, restore its ruins, and build it as it used to be.

Are you feeling broken or run down today and in need of restoration? Do you need rebuilding and restoring to your former glory? Are there some broken places hidden deep inside you that no one else knows about?

Come to the Master Restorer today and hand yourself over to Him – for just as God promised to restore David's fallen tent, so he promises to restore you!

You need to put yourself completely into the Lord's hands – every fragile and hurting part – trusting that he knows exactly how to repair you, what needs to be done and how long it will take. Trust him today – hand everything over to Him and wait and see what God will make of you!

O Sovereign Lord, how I need you to come and restore me! I choose this day to give you every part of me, ask you to mend those broken places that only you and I know about and to restore me to my former glory – ALL for Your glory! Amen.

02 OCTOBER

Sowing and Reaping

Obadiah v 15: The day of the LORD is near for all nations. As you have done, it will be done to you; your deeds will return upon your own head.

God spoke these words to Obadiah concerning Edom, but all nations are to be included in the Lord's final judgement. If all the bad things they had done would eventually come upon them, then it is equally true that, if they had done good things instead, good deeds would have come upon them!

I don't know about you, but after reading this I feel very inspired to carry out good deeds, especially towards my fellow man. It is worth reminding ourselves that nothing we do goes unnoticed by God, he sees every little thing and he also hears every little thought! So, if I am acting badly towards others, either in thought, word or deed, people will start behaving badly towards me; but if I have loving and forgiving thoughts and speak and act kindly towards others, I will find that people are far more likely to be kind to me, and my ultimate reward will be in God.

O Lord, although I knew of this law, that I will reap what I sow, I thank you for highlighting it for me today and may I take any necessary steps I need, in order to gain a better harvest! Amen.

03 OCTOBER

What Are You Running From?

Jonah 1 v 3: But Jonah ran away from the LORD and headed for Tarshish.

What makes us run? Fear? Hurt? Anger? Rebellion? In Jonah's case it was rebellion; he plain and simply didn't want to do what God was asking him to and so he ran! Elijah ran too, but he ran in fear for his life as Jezebel had threatened to kill him! I wonder, are you possibly running from something today?

Amazingly, in both Jonah's and Elijah's cases, God met them and rescued them from the situations they had run into! Jonah is saved from drowning in the sea and Elijah from dying in the desert and they both receive instructions on what to do next! And so, if this is you today, if you are running, either from something or someone, then please know this – the Lord will find you and he will rescue you from whatever mess you have got yourself into, and he will show you clearly what to do next.

Heavenly Father, I'm sorry for the times I run, especially when I run from you. Sometimes I don't even know why I'm running, but you do and will always come to find me, save me and put me back on the right pathway. Thank you for being willing to give me a second chance! Amen.

04 OCTOBER

Life-Giving Words

Micah 2 v 7: ... Do not my words do good to him whose ways are upright?

Never underestimate the power of God's words, especially for those of us who believe! If only we fully realised all the good they could do for us, I am sure we would make much more room in our daily lives to study them, just as we make room for other things that do us good.

Unlike other books, God's word is alive – it can speak to us today, directly into our current situations. This is what makes it so very exciting to me! God has spoken to me about quite detailed things at times through his word, at just the right time! This is the main way in which God speaks to us and shows his concern over every detail of our life. Why would we not want to read it more?

Please forgive me Lord for neglecting to spend as much time in your word as I could. Only you know the blessings I am missing out on, when I turn instead to other things. Please help me Lord, to hear your voice. Amen.

05 OCTOBER

God's Heart

Micah 6 v 8: He has showed you, O man, what is good. And what does the LORD require of you? To act justly and to love mercy and to walk humbly with your God.

Today I believe we are looking directly into the heart of God. He is showing us here what is really important to him and telling us how he wants us to behave. Three special things really matter to God: Justice, Mercy and Humility. If we display these traits in our lives we show that we have the heart of our Father – that we are walking in His ways!

These traits may come naturally to some of us. We may find some easier than others, but I believe God wants us to have all three, as it will be a witness to the people around us that we are indeed children of God! His heart can then be seen and shared with others.

How much do I need to change?

Your heart, O Lord, is so tender and merciful; please humble me and soften any hardness that still remains in my own. You know what needs to be done Lord; I give you permission to carry out any necessary heart surgery! Amen.

06 OCTOBER

Prepare Your Defences!

Nahum 3 v 14: Draw water for the siege, strengthen your defences! Work the clay, tread the mortar, repair the brickwork!

There will be times in our lives when we will be clearly under enemy attack and it will do us no good at all if we wait until the attack occurs to build our defences – we need to be ready, alert and have our forms of defence in place long before we are attacked or under siege!

Our war is spiritual and so we need to have our spiritual forms of defence at the ready! We need to know who we are in Christ – a righteous child of God. We need to keep our faith and trust in God strong by regularly exercising them in our everyday lives, and we need to know God's word, so that we can speak it out against the enemy when he comes to us with his lies! We also need the water of his word to sustain us through the trial. If we do all these things we will be ready for anything, in and through Christ!

Thank you Lord, for you have richly provided me with everything I need to defend myself against the enemy, but help me to make sure I am fully prepared. Amen.

07 OCTOBER
Lord Have Mercy

Habakkuk 3 v 2: LORD, I have heard of your fame; I stand in awe of your deeds, O LORD. Renew them in our day, in our time make them known; in wrath remember mercy.

Can you relate to Habakkuk's prayer here? He is living in desperate times. People need to repent of their sin and turn back to God, but they are blissfully unaware of how much they are hurting the Lord, and if they continue in their ways they will bring about God's ultimate judgement on them. Habakkuk is standing in the gap here; he is crying out to God, asking him to show mercy; he is interceding for the people!

Habakkuk's cry is also that God may once again reveal himself, by his great deeds. O how we need God to reveal himself today in our land! Is God maybe calling you to intercede on behalf of the people where you live? How we need to cry out for God to have mercy in these times!

O Sovereign Lord, today we cry out to you for mercy; please hold back your wrath from this nation and make your great deeds known to us again in our day! Amen.

08 OCTOBER

O What a Song!

Zephaniah 3 v 17: The LORD your God is with you, he is mighty to save. He will take great delight in you, he will quiet you with his love, he will rejoice over you with singing.

I don't know about you, but these words are almost too much to take in! In fact, it might be a good idea to quietly read them over again, meditating on each amazing truth!

Did you still find it hard to take in the richness of God's love for you? I confess I still do! Maybe if this is you as well, it might be a good idea for us to read this verse regularly until it does fully sink in. Why not write it out and place it somewhere where you can easily read it each day.

God delights in you so much; he is with you and for you and longs to quiet you with his love and He is singing over you – such is His joy over you! What other song could we possibly need to hear?

Thank you Lord for loving me, and thank you for guiding Zephaniah to share this truth about your love for us – please help me to fully take it in! Amen.

09 OCTOBER

All Stirred Up!

Haggai 1 v 14: So the LORD stirred up the spirit of Zerubbabel son of Shealtiel, governor of Judah, and the spirit of Joshua son of Jehozadak, the high priest, and the spirit of the whole remnant of the people. They came and began work on the house of the LORD Almighty, their God...

Isn't it encouraging to know that when God wants us to do something for him he actually stirs us up from within, so that we are eager to get on with the task in hand. So if you find that what you're doing for the Lord is a laborious chore and like pushing a dead weight uphill, I would seriously question whether the Lord still wants you doing this? Not that the Lord's work is always easy, but I believe there will be an underlying incentive, and even joy in doing it, despite the difficulties that may arise along the way!

The verse today also shows us that when our Lord wants something done, he knows just who to choose to do it!

Please guide me Lord, show me if I am clinging onto work for you that you are now finished with, and stir me up to do the new thing you have prepared for me! Amen.

10 OCTOBER

From Rags to Riches

Zechariah 3 v 4: The angel said to those who were standing before him, "Take off his filthy clothes." Then he said to Joshua, "See, I have taken away your sin, and I will put rich garments on you."

Imagine yourself as Joshua, the high priest, standing there before the Lord, wearing disgustingly dirty clothes – ashamed and completely exposed! Added to all this, Satan is right there too, ready to accuse you before God (see verses 1 & 2). How does this make you feel? Hold that thought. Now imagine the Lord himself stepping in to defend you. He rebukes Satan and then commands that your filthy rags be removed and you be dressed in the richest of garments! How do you feel now?

I hope that exercise proved helpful and has made you aware of all that God has done for you. What a turn-around - from your lowest point of shame and degradation to suddenly being lifted to a place of utter well-being and safety! And this was all instigated by God. Why do we worry and fear so, when we clearly have God on our side?

O Father, all I can do is say, 'Thank You', and yet that hardly seems enough after all you have done for me. But I say it from the bottom of my heart. Amen.

11 OCTOBER

Be My Spirit

Zechariah 4 v 6: ... This is the word of the LORD to Zerubbabel: 'Not by might nor by power, but by my Spirit,' says the LORD Almighty.

This verse is pretty well-known among Christians, but I felt it was worth taking a look at today.

In our world where self-sufficiency rules, it is so easy to forget that we have it all the wrong way round! God created us to need Him; we are designed to work best if we first seek God for our needs each day. Not only will he supply all our needs, but will also provide the strength and wisdom we need to carry out whatever our tasks are to be. Likewise, if we come up against a difficulty, we may be tempted to try and bulldoze our way through it in our own strength – then we wonder why we still have the problem!

God's Word for you today is 'Not by might or by power but by My Spirit.' Try it and see!

Please forgive me Father for trying to do everything in my own strength. May I give you control of each day before it gets started and ask for your Spirit to help me in everything I do. Amen.

12 OCTOBER

God's Special People

Zechariah 8 v 23: ... In those days ten men from all languages and nations will take firm hold of one Jew by the hem of his robe and say, "Let us go with you, because we have heard that God is with you."

This is only one of many scriptures that shows us how 'special' the Jews are to God - they are his chosen ones as are we, now that we have been grafted in (see Romans 11 v 17-18).

All believers are one in Christ, but our roots are in the Jewish nation. Just as people recognised that God was with the Jews, many people also recognise that God is with us! Others may want what we have and desire to follow us in order to find God - for we have the words of Eternal Life! And who wouldn't want that?

Dear Lord, thank you for our Jewish brothers; we recognise the special place they hold within your heart and long for them to come to know Jesus as their Messiah. May the veil be removed from their eyes O Lord, so that they can see who you truly are; and may I remember to pray for them. Amen.

13 OCTOBER

Our Humble King

Zechariah 9 v 9: Rejoice greatly, O Daughter of Zion! Shout, Daughter of Jerusalem! See, your king comes to you, righteous and having salvation, gentle and riding on a donkey, on a colt, the foal of a donkey.

We have the privilege of living on the other side of this prophetic word, but how strange it would have sounded to the people of Israel as they read it – a king coming on a donkey, and a colt at that! Surely that couldn't be right? I have no doubt it was soon pushed far from their minds, otherwise they would've recognised the day when this word was fulfilled in every minute detail! That is the thing with prophetic words, there is so much detail in them that it should be obvious to us when they come to pass.

I wonder, are we listening to what God's prophets are telling us Today? Are we heeding their warnings? Just as the Jews didn't see their Messiah when he came; are we missing something too?

Your prophetic words are amazing Lord. Thank you for describing our Lord's entry into Jerusalem in such detail – that he rode not just on a donkey, but on a colt! May we take your prophetic words seriously and hear what you are saying to your Church today! Amen.

14 OCTOBER

Missed Blessing?

Malachi 3 v 10: "Bring the whole tithe into the storehouse, that there may be food in my house. Test me in this," says the LORD Almighty, "and see if I will not throw open the floodgates of heaven and pour out so much blessing that you will not have room enough for it."

Everything we have comes from God. It is not our own, and the practice of giving God the first ten per cent of everything we are given reminds us of this fact. If we love and trust God we should be more than happy to tithe, especially as in doing so we know God promises to bless us beyond measure, as today's verse so clearly tells us. So why is it so many of us struggle to do this?

Our God is a giving God – for "God so loved the World that he gave…" and as His children, we should be like him – longing to give! Who knows what blessings we may have missed out on, simply because we didn't give to God. Not that we 'give to get', that should never be our motive for giving – for it should always come from a heart full of love, eager to please God and wanting to give back to Him!

O Lord, after all you have given me, how could I withhold anything from you? Please forgive me Father and stir me up to give and then to keep on giving! Amen.

15 OCTOBER

Love Always Covers

Matthew 1 v 19: Because Joseph her husband was a righteous man and did not want to expose her to public disgrace, he had in mind to divorce her quietly.

I don't know about you, but I have always marvelled at this verse because I believe it shows us the heart of God. Joseph could have become angry with Mary and thrown her out for getting pregnant by someone else, but he didn't. Instead, he cared for her in a kind and loving manner as he didn't want her situation to be publicly exposed. He was concerned and planned to cover her disgrace (not that she had actually done anything wrong).

Love always protects, that is its very nature. Likewise God is love and He always protects! God knew Joseph's heart and he specifically chose him to be the earthly father to his Son. God certainly knew what he was doing!

I now ask myself, "How often am I guilty of exposing others' faults?" It can be so easy to judge others rather than act in love and keep their misdeeds quiet.

Thank you Father, that you do not treat us as our sins deserve. Please help me to be equally forbearing with other people's misdeeds. Amen.

16 OCTOBER

Forgiveness

Matthew 6 v 15: But if you do not forgive men their sins, your Father will not forgive your sins.

Forgiving those that have hurt us is such a powerful and important aspect of Christian living. We so often overlook it, preferring instead to hold on to our un-forgiveness, while assuming the Lord will still forgive us - but he doesn't!

Our heavenly Father understands how hard it is. He had to watch men crucify his one and only Son, and yet Jesus asked his Father to forgive them, for they knew not what they were doing - and people quite often don't!

There is such freedom and blessing when you choose to forgive. While you refuse to forgive someone, you remain tethered to the hurt, but once you forgive, you are set free and can receive God's forgiveness and fully enjoy all the blessings he has for you. Why not try it and see? It doesn't mean that what they did was right - God will be their judge - but if you forgive, it will release you from bondage!

O Lord, please help me to forgive like you do. Forgive me for holding on to all this bitterness and resentment. I choose this day to forgive! Amen.

17 OCTOBER

Put the Words in My Mouth

Matthew 10 v 19-20: But when they arrest you, do not worry about what to say or how to say it. At that time you will be given what to say, for it will not be you speaking, but the Spirit of your Father speaking through you.

This is such a helpful and comforting verse to know, especially when we find our back is up against a wall and our power of speech has deserted us! Have you ever been in that kind of situation before? Maybe you are in one now?

When under pressure. we often panic and say the very first thing that pops into our head, without first waiting on God's lead and guidance. I encourage you to press the pause button next time you have a difficult or challenging situation to sort out, then pray and ask for God's Spirit to speak through you in this situation. You'll be amazed at the result!

Thank you Father for giving me Your words through your Holy Spirit. May I tune in to them not only during a crisis but at all times during my everyday life. Amen.

18 OCTOBER

Yoked to Freedom

Matthew 11 v 29: Take my yoke upon you and learn from me, for I am gentle and humble in heart, and you will find rest for your souls.

I really wanted to include the verses on either side of this one as I think they are some of the most life-changing if we really take them in and follow them. I would encourage you to meditate on them, and read them in different versions of the Bible too!

Jesus is advising us to come to him and allow ourselves to be yoked to him so that we might find rest. But isn't a yoke rather restricting? I won't be free! How can my soul find rest when I am trapped like this? All understandable concerns - if we were talking of a 'normal' yoking - but being yoked to Jesus will be completely the opposite, for his yoke is light and not burdensome at all. We will become freer than we ever have been when we become joined to him! Can you imagine the security this would bring? God won't put anything heavy on you; if you feel heaviness it hasn't come from Him!

Thank you Lord, for showing me that Your yoke is a delight to wear and it will give me a sense of being free rather than trapped; may I take it upon myself now. Amen.

19 OCTOBER

Take Up Your Cross

Matthew 16 v 24: Then Jesus said to his disciples, "If anyone would come after me, he must deny himself and take up his cross and follow me."

This verse, at first glance, may look rather daunting; after all, who wants to deny themselves? Generally speaking, we would all like to lead lives full of comfort without any pain or suffering – but then they wouldn't be satisfying or rewarding lives, because we wouldn't be with Jesus.

Even Jesus himself didn't want to die on a cross, but he did want to please his Father in heaven, rather than please himself. He knew that dying in this way would lead to his ultimate joy; the salvation of many souls. No one said it would be easy, but there is still amazing peace to be found, even in the midst of pain and suffering, whenever you decide to follow Jesus!

I confess Lord Jesus that my flesh, just as yours did, shrinks back from the idea of suffering. Please help me to be prepared to say, like you – 'Your will be done Lord, not mine!' Amen.

20 OCTOBER

Love Challenge

Matthew 25 v 40: The King will reply, "I tell you the truth, whatever you did for one of the least of these brothers of mine, you did for me."

Here, in one of his well-known parables, Jesus lets us know that God is fully aware of how we treat people, and he shows us just how important this is to him and for our future life too (read Matthew 5 v 31-46). If we held this teaching at the forefront of our mind, I believe it would revolutionise how we treat other people.

It is mind-blowing when you realise that the person you have just spoken rudely to - was in fact 'Jesus'!!! Whatever we do to another we are doing to Jesus. It is very sobering and probably one of the most challenging parables.

But just think how we can bless Jesus if we care for those who are less fortunate than us, or who are alone or unwell in hospital or in prison. May we become far more aware of the needs around us and respond in brotherly love.

My heart is broken, now that I realise just how often I have hurt you Lord Jesus, without even realising it. Please help me to remember that everything I do to others, I do to you! Amen.

21 OCTOBER

The Way Made Open

Matthew 27 v 51: At that moment the curtain of the temple was torn in two from top to bottom.

According to Matthew the curtain was torn as Jesus gave up his spirit. The curtain was between the Holy place where the priests ministered and the Holy of Holies where God's presence was. No one could enter, except the high priest once a year on the 'Day of Atonement'.

The curtain being torn is such a powerful picture of what Jesus achieved on the cross. The way to God is now open to everyone who believes in what Jesus has done, and it is God who has torn the curtain - as it was torn from the top! No more sacrifices for sin are needed. Jesus has paid the price for all of us, by being the perfect sacrifice once and for all!

We can now enter boldly into the Holy of Holies, straight into the presence of our God – what a privilege! We don't need to go through any rituals, as now we can come in the name of Jesus, by his precious blood that was shed for us!

O Father, how I thank you that the way has been made open for me to come and kneel at your feet, where I am able to tell you what is on my heart and to hear what is on yours; surely there is no greater thing! Amen.

22 OCTOBER

What a Promise!

Matthew 28 v 20: … And surely I am with you always, to the very end of the age.

What a splendid way to end this gospel - on such a positive note! These may be very familiar words to us, but do we really believe them? If we truly believed them we wouldn't worry, we would have no fear for the future and we would feel at peace and very safe and secure. If Jesus has promised to be with us always, then we are never alone during any of life's dramas. This is why Jesus got so upset with his disciples during the storm – because although he was with them in the boat, they still became afraid! The disciples didn't really trust Jesus, even though they had seen him perform miracles and healing.

If Jesus has promised to be with you always then Jesus will be with you always! Never doubt it for one moment; however bad things may look – He is there! Just reach out and take hold of His hand!

O Lord, please forgive me when I fail to recognise that you are right there with me in every single situation. Even when it doesn't feel like it, You are still there holding my hand. Thank you so much for never leaving me. Amen.

23 OCTOBER

Another Baptism

Mark 1 v 8: I baptise you with water, but he will baptise you with the Holy Spirit.

John the Baptist made it plain that the one coming after him was far greater than he, and that this one would baptise them with the Holy Spirit! For those listening, this would have been hard to understand and I think a lot of us still struggle with this concept today – God's Holy Spirit actually coming to live inside me?

'Baptise' means to completely immerse and just as the people were immersed in the water, so would they be immersed with the Holy Spirit. You cannot be completely immersed without knowing about it, and when the Holy Spirit comes upon you, you will be aware of His presence entering your body, as he comes gently, like a dove, and fills every part of you with an overwhelming sense of His love, joy and peace. His presence gives you all you need to change and become more like Jesus.

Please forgive me Lord for being apprehensive about being filled with your Spirit. Why would I be afraid when He is Your Spirit? I am willing and ready to receive him. Please baptise me with your Holy Spirit. Fill me now, so that I may be equipped to do all you ask of me. Amen.

24 OCTOBER

Who Needs a Doctor?

Mark 2 v 17: On hearing this, Jesus said to them, "It is not the healthy who need a doctor, but the sick. I have not come to call the righteous, but sinners."

The religious leaders of the day believed they were right with God because they kept all the rules, but in reality their hearts weren't right towards God or towards others. This is why they were questioning Jesus about his eating with sinners and tax collectors. They were blind to their own faults and didn't recognise their own needs, so Jesus tells them he hasn't come for the 'righteous'. Oh, but look at his loving and open heart towards the sinners. He has come to help and set them free from the bondage that sin inevitably brings with it. Just like a doctor, he has come to heal them and bind up their wounds.

Jesus is here for you today – right now - and he longs to minister to you, whatever your need is. We all have needs; we may not like to admit it – but we do! Just ask 'doctor' Jesus to make you better today, accept his instructions and take his medicine – for you will feel all the better for it, I promise you!

Thank you Lord Jesus - you care for sinners. Please forgive me all of my sins and heal me today. Amen.

25 OCTOBER

Let Jesus Calm Your Storm

Mark 4 v 39: He got up, rebuked the wind and said to the waves, "Quiet! Be still!" Then the wind died down and it was completely calm.

Imagine being in that boat at that moment; one minute there are these enormous waves crashing over into the boat – it is absolutely terrifying - and the next, after Jesus has spoken to the storm it is still and quiet, just like a millpond. Wow! Can you sense the utter amazement the disciples must have felt? They had never seen anything like it! Jesus had spoken to the storm and it had obeyed him!

Now imagine that you're going through some great inner turmoil, full of anxiety, stress and even outright panic. You feel totally unable to control it – not unlike that great storm. Now stop and speak to those feelings, command them to 'Be Still' in Jesus Name! And keep doing it, fully believing that Jesus can calm that storm within you – because he can!

Thank you Lord Jesus, you speak and it comes to pass. Please help me to remember the power of your Word and that you are master over every storm. I believe that as I speak your Word, you can calm my inner storm. Amen.

26 OCTOBER

Childlike Trust

Mark 10 v 15: I tell you the truth, anyone who will not receive the kingdom of God like a little child will never enter it.

Generally speaking, little children have no worries; they trust their parents to feed and clothe them and to take care of them if they are unwell. They ask for help when they need it without any sense of shame or embarrassment. I believe these are the qualities that Jesus is looking for in his followers; he wants us to approach our heavenly Father in a similar manner – with genuine childlike trust!

As a child is dependent upon its parents for everything it needs, so God wants us to be dependent upon Him for everything we need. This can be easier for some of us than others. It involves us realising we are not in charge of our life and neither are we capable of looking after ourselves, which is very humbling indeed. We tend to be independent and self-sufficient by nature - taking pride in what we can achieve in our own strength.

O Heavenly Father, it's so wonderful to know you are looking after me and yet it's hard to give up my independence. Please help me become more childlike in my relationship with you.
Amen.

27 OCTOBER

Faith Moves Mountains

Mark 11 v 23: I tell you the truth, if anyone says to this mountain, "Go, throw yourself into the sea," and does not doubt in his heart but believes that what he says will happen, it will be done for him.

What an earth-moving scripture this is (excuse the pun)! I found it mind-boggling when I sat and really thought about the possibility of a huge mountain falling into the sea.

What 'mountain' do you need shifting in your life today? Maybe you have several? If you take the Lord Jesus at his word here and command it to go in his name, without doubting, then it will be done for you!

I confess I have found this verse very challenging indeed; doubts tend to crowd into my thinking uninvited. Maybe it would be a good idea for us to meditate on our Lord's words before us today, to allow them to fully sink in so that we can really believe them.

O Lord, I want to believe this so much; please help me to fully take it in. Mountains will move - for nothing is impossible for you. Amen.

28 OCTOBER

A Willing Spirit

Luke 1 v 38: "I am the Lord's servant," Mary answered. "May it be to me as you have said." Then the angel left her.

What an amazingly quick response to the stunning news and visitation that Mary had just received! I would still have been in utter shock and disbelief. But God knew why he was choosing Mary to be the mother of his Son. Among her many other qualities, Mary had a willing spirit; she just wanted to be obedient unto the Lord and saw herself as his maidservant and nothing more. This surely is one of the main reasons Mary was chosen!

God is still looking for people like Mary today; those who will unquestionably do as he asks them; those who long to follow his instructions and live in His will, rather than wanting their own way. God longs for all of his children to have a willing spirit and to see them fulfilling the wonderful plans that he has for their lives – if only they will submit to him!

O Father, please forgive me that I so often prefer living my way rather than yours, yet whenever I submit to you, my life is always so much sweeter for it. Why would I ever choose my way rather than yours? Amen.

29 OCTOBER

Reach Out!

Luke 6 v 19: … and the people all tried to touch him, because power was coming from him and healing them all.

We don't hear quite so much about the healing ministry of Jesus these days as we do about his preaching ministry, but the two go very much hand in hand. God's word is still preached, and God still heals today. We not only need to believe this, we also need to reach out and receive it - just as all the people around Jesus did.

What holds us back? Maybe it's the fear of not being healed? And yet we have nothing to lose. The worst that can happen is nothing and even if that does happen, where does it say that we can't go on asking and asking and asking?

Jesus' word to you today is, 'Do not be afraid; believe in me; reach out and touch me; your faith has healed you.'

Lord Jesus, I come to you today, confessing my doubts and yet longing to fully believe you. Just as those around you reached out to receive your healing power – so now, I too reach out in faith and receive your healing power. Amen.

30 OCTOBER

Let Your Light Shine

Luke 8 v 16: No-one lights a lamp and hides it in a jar or puts it under a bed. Instead, he puts it on a stand, so that those who come in can see the light.

Our Christian faith was never meant to be a 'private' matter, as today's verse so clearly illustrates. Jesus tells us that we should be 'lights' for everyone to see and others should be able to see the difference in us. Jesus should be shining out of us, in the ways that we act and behave towards other people.

Those coming into the Christian faith need to be able to see our light in order to see their way ahead, otherwise they will be tripping up, stumbling and falling on their Christian journey. We all have a responsibility not to hide our faith away, but to bring it out into the open!

O Lord, I thank you and praise you for giving us this vivid picture of how our faith needs to show. May I be willing to share what I have with others and be as you would be unto them, so they in turn can walk in the light; no longer stumbling around in the darkness. Amen.

31 OCTOBER

Going the Extra Mile

Luke 10 v 35: The next day he took out two silver coins and gave them to the innkeeper. "Look after him," he said, "and when I return, I will reimburse you for any extra expense you may have."

'The Good Samaritan' is one of my favourite parables; it never fails to warm my heart. First there is the stark contrast between how this poor man (who has just been beaten up and left for dead) is treated – initially being completely ignored by two people and then suddenly receiving the most tender and loving care. Secondly, this 'good' Samaritan shows such radical kindness by going above and beyond what he needed to. He pays for him to be looked after and cared for until he is fully recovered.

This is how God wants us to love others, with the same radical kindness as this 'good' Samaritan - always willing to go the extra mile, even to the point where it may cost us dearly.

Heavenly Father, please help me to be as radical with my kindness as the Samaritan was in this story. May I no longer be happy with doing the least I can get by with, but only be content when I do my utmost! Amen.

01 NOVEMBER

The Father's Love

Luke 15 v 20: ... But while he was still a long way off, his father saw him and was filled with compassion for him; he ran to his son, threw his arms around him and kissed him.

The wayward son, now destitute and longing to eat pig swill, realises that even his father's servants are better off than he is, so he decides to go back home, apologise to his father and ask if he can become one of his servants. Imagine how the son is feeling as he makes that long walk home. Now imagine his utter amazement as he sees his father running towards him, with his arms outstretched, no doubt with tears of joy streaming down his face, and then before he can make his request known, his father is throwing his arms around him and kissing him!

This is how much Father God loves you – no matter how far you've strayed, no matter what you have done – you are still his beloved child and he loves you! And when you return to him, he will always run out to welcome you – throwing his loving arms around you once again!

Thank you Father, that you love me so much; even though I don't deserve it. Please forgive me for ever leaving your side. O how I long to be back in your arms again. Amen.

02 NOVEMBER

Persistence Pays

Luke 18 v 5: … yet because this widow keeps bothering me, I will see that she gets justice, so that she won't eventually wear me out with her coming!

Jesus taught his disciples this parable to encourage them to never give up in prayer. The judge in this parable had no intention of helping this widow to get justice, as he neither feared God or men. However, because the widow kept on coming to him time after time, pestering him with the same request over and over again it caused him to grant her request, even despite his total lack of care or concern for her.

Be encouraged if you have been praying about something for a long time – don't ever give up for your answer could well be just around the next corner. God wants us to keep asking, to keep knocking and to keep seeking – and if an unjust judge answered this widow's request, how much more will your loving heavenly Father answer yours!

O Lord, you know how challenging prayer can be for me at times, and how easily I falter and give up. Please help me to focus and be motivated to keep on praying, even though I cannot see anything changing. I trust that you are already working behind the scenes. Amen.

03 NOVEMBER

He Sees You

Luke 19 v 5: When Jesus reached the spot, he looked up and said to him, "Zacchaeus, come down immediately. I must stay at your house today."

What a reward Zacchaeus received that day for wanting to see Jesus. Being so short he had climbed a tree so that he could see Jesus passing by. He must have almost fallen out of the tree in surprise when Jesus stopped right beneath him and spoke his name - asking him to come down because he was coming home with him! Zaccheaus would not have expected Jesus to notice him let alone speak to him or come home with him – but Jesus saw him that day and he sees you too!

This same Jesus wants to stop beneath your tree, so to speak, and say the very same thing to you – 'I must come to your house today!' With Jesus sitting next to you in your living room it would soon become apparent what you needed to put right in your life, just as it did for Zacchaeus! Jesus knows everything about you and he sees you wherever you are, even if you happen to be up a tree!

O Lord Jesus, there is nothing that escapes your notice! I am glad you see me and are interested enough to want to help me change and become a better person. I welcome you to come home with me today Lord. Amen.

04 NOVEMBER

The Choice is Yours

Luke 23 v 41: We are punished justly, for we are getting what our deeds deserve. But this man has done nothing wrong.

These words were uttered by one of the two thieves crucified on either side of Jesus. This thief could see that Jesus was an innocent man, and was indeed the 'King of the Jews' - because he then said, 'Jesus, remember me when you come into your kingdom.'

It has always struck me that both thieves had the same experience, and yet one chose to believe and follow Jesus and the other man didn't, but continued cursing and swearing as he hung there in agony. I often wonder whether the repentant thief noticed the pain a little less, now that he knew he would soon be in paradise. Every person has this same choice - to either believe in Jesus or reject Jesus. Which do you choose?

Thank you Lord Jesus, that even as death approached, you were still willing to reach out and save; yes, even a criminal deserving to die, for such is your great love and compassion! I pray for all those who don't yet know you, that their eyes may be opened, like the thief on the cross, so they can see who you really are – the Son of God; may they cry out to you and be saved! Amen.

05 NOVEMBER

Do Whatever He Tells You

John 2 v 5: His mother said to the servants, "Do whatever he tells you."

Most people have heard about Jesus turning water into wine at a Wedding to save the host from public humiliation, but do we ever think about the servants' role in this? First, the servants had to believe in Mary's words - to do whatever Jesus told them to do and secondly, they had to act upon what he told them to do, no matter how impossible or difficult it appeared to them. They had to take the water to the master of the banquet to taste, trusting that Jesus would come through for them before it reached his lips! If they hadn't followed Jesus' instructions, there would have been no more wine at the wedding, that day!

If you'd like your life to be turned from one of 'water' into 'wine', then a great starting point would be believing what you 'hear' and then doing whatever Jesus asks of you, no matter what it takes or how impossible it looks. No 'ifs' or 'buts', just total obedience and trust in Him.

O Lord, what faith and trust those servants had in You, it puts my own to shame. Please help me to become bolder in stepping out in faith, as you lead me. Amen.

317

06 NOVEMBER

Do You Want to Get Well?

John 5 v 6: When Jesus saw him lying there and learned that he had been in this condition for a long time, he asked him, "Do you want to get well?"

What strikes you when you first read this? Well surely the answer would be 'yes' if he's lying near the 'healing' pool; this shows he wants to get well, doesn't it? So why did Jesus ask him if he wanted to get well?

I wonder, is there a message hidden here for us today? Is Jesus maybe showing us that he needs our willingness in order for us to receive our healing? Maybe deep down, we would miss all the attention and support which we now receive for being unwell? Maybe the idea of being thrust back into living a normal life scares us slightly? We are so used to being this way and there is a degree of comfort in the familiar. And then what if I get my hopes up and Jesus doesn't heal me? All these are well founded thoughts and questions – and yet, if we truly want to be healed I believe none of these will matter. That is what Jesus is looking for – just our simple childlike faith and trust in Him for our healing. So why not ask Him now?

O Lord Jesus, I come to you now, truly wanting to be healed, and I ask that you cleanse and heal me, in your most precious name. Amen.

07 NOVEMBER

Who Are We to Judge?

John 8 v 7: When they kept on questioning him, he straightened up and said to them, "If any one of you is without sin, let him be the first to throw a stone at her."

Imagine how petrified and ashamed this woman, caught in the very act of adultery, must have felt and how confident, puffed up and clever the religious leaders, who had brought her before Jesus also felt in trying to catch him out! But wait - Jesus was just about to change all that!

We may be familiar with Jesus' words in today's verse, and yet they never fail to amaze me. What an impact they must have had when first spoken! The proud leaders gradually walk away, because not one of them is without sin; not one of them has the right to judge this woman. Only Jesus can do that and yet he forgives the woman and tells her to leave her life of sin.

Likewise, we have no right to judge our fellow man when we ourselves are so far from perfect, for we all fall short; but Jesus is still here willing to forgive us today.

Forgive me Father, for the many times I have judged others; how dare I, when I am so in need of your forgiveness myself? Thank you for forgiving me. Amen.

08 NOVEMBER

Hear My Voice

John 10 v 27: My sheep listen to my voice; I know them, and they follow me.

This analogy, of Jesus as our shepherd and us as his sheep, is really wonderful - it teaches us so much while comforting us at the same time. For anyone out there who may still be a little sceptical about being able to hear Jesus speak to you, I thoroughly recommend reading the whole section in John 10 about the shepherd and his flock.

So how do we hear our Lord speak to us? The most common way is through reading the bible. But how do we know when he is talking personally to us? As we read, certain words will speak into our hearts, and we will have an insight as to what they mean in relation to our lives at that time. For example, let's say we are reading about Peter getting out of the boat and walking on the water. We may realise as we read, that Jesus is calling us to step out in faith, into something new, which might appear rather challenging to us. And just as Jesus saved Peter from sinking, so will he be there to help us in our struggles. This is what makes the Christian life so exciting – our Saviour is alive and wants to speak to us!

Dear Lord Jesus, please will you help me to hear your voice, especially as I read your word. Amen.

09 NOVEMBER

Why Delay?

John 11 v 6: Yet when he heard that Lazarus was sick, he stayed where he was two more days.

Jesus only did what his heavenly Father told him to do, so when he stayed where he was for two more days, rather than rushing to Lazarus's sick bed to heal him, we know that he was following his Father's instructions. How hurtful and confusing this must have appeared! Imagine how deserted Mary and Martha, Lazarus's sisters, would have felt; they must have thought that Jesus didn't care. Little did they know that there was a purpose and plan in all this, which would bring about even greater glory to God - to raise Lazarus from the dead!

I find this account a great comfort when I don't understand why God isn't answering my prayers or why someone I love is suffering so much. God hasn't forgotten us - he has a bigger purpose here! He knows what he is doing, so trust him completely - even when it makes no sense at all!

Thank you Father that your ways are always perfect, and far above mine. You know exactly what you are doing and I believe it will all work out for Your Glory and also for my ultimate good; so I choose to leave it all with you this day. Amen.

10 NOVEMBER

A Place for You

John 14 v 2: In my Father's house are many rooms; if it were not so, I would have told you. I am going there to prepare a place for you.

Isn't this verse just incredible when you really stop and think about it! We won't just be floating around aimlessly in heaven, because Jesus has already gone on ahead to get a special place ready for us!

We are all very individual with different interests and personalities, and I believe these will all still exist in heaven. You will still be what makes you, 'you' and I will still be what makes me, 'me', apart from any sinful or negative aspects of course!

What care and attention to detail the Lord has for us, that he even wants to give some insight into our 'forever' home! It makes me so thrilled to think of Jesus getting a place ready especially for me, along with the excitement of wondering what he will have chosen for me. How about you?

Thank you Lord Jesus, for loving me so much; I am in awe, quite frankly, of all you have in store for me and I can't wait to be with you forever! Amen.

11 NOVEMBER

Peace in Troubled Times

John 16 v 33: I have told you these things, so that in me you may have peace. In this world you will have trouble. But take heart! I have overcome the world.

Contrary to popular belief Jesus never promised us a trouble-free life, and if anyone says becoming a Christian means all your troubles will be over – they are lying! However, with Jesus in our life we have someone with us who is always there to help us through these tough times, because he has promised to be with us and he has promised to give us His 'peace', yes, even during our trials!

Maybe you're in a terrible situation right now? Or maybe the world situation is overwhelming you? If so, instead of stressing over it or complaining about it, may I encourage you to try trusting the Lord Jesus with it, knowing that He is right there in the midst of it all. Just hand everything over to him and receive His 'peace'. Remember, Jesus is far greater than anything this world can throw at you!

Dear Lord Jesus, I am so grateful that you are aware of all the troubles in this world and that you not only care, but have already overcome them. I receive your 'peace', even in the midst of these troubled times, because I know you are with me. Amen.

12 NOVEMBER

Power to Witness

Acts 1 v 8: But you will receive power when the Holy Spirit comes on you; and you will be my witnesses in Jerusalem, and in all Judea and Samaria, and to the ends of the earth.

I am so grateful that Jesus didn't just leave us to our own devices and capabilities, but that he provided us with the power and boldness to witness for him, by sending His Holy Spirit. He didn't leave us to try and figure it out on our own or to try to do it in our own strength. No, He has fully equipped us for the task before us and as long as we remember that we need His help and ask the Holy Spirit to guide and strengthen us we can't go wrong!

Perhaps asking the Holy Spirit to come and help has never occurred to you before; maybe you find witnessing to others a real struggle? Jesus never meant for it to be a struggle; that is why he sent His Spirit to be our Helper. If you have never received the Holy Spirit's power, why not ask Him to come and fill you now?

O Lord Jesus, how I thank you that I no longer need to struggle to try and witness for you. Please fill me with your Holy Spirit that I may go forth in your power! Amen.

13 NOVEMBER

What Do You Have?

Acts 3 v 6: Then Peter said, "Silver or gold I do not have, but what I have I give you. In the name of Jesus Christ of Nazareth, walk."

Some of us may feel we have nothing much to offer in God's service, or that we are far too insignificant to do anything substantial for God; but how far from the truth this is! As believers in Jesus Christ, we have been given authority in His name, to do all that He did and even greater things (see John 14 v 12)! Jesus has made all the resources of the kingdom of heaven available to us and he expects us to use them!

I hope this isn't making you feel condemned, but rather excited at the prospect of what you can do in and through His name! And just as Jesus only did what he saw His Father doing, so too must we only do what God shows us to do.

Dear Heavenly Father, although at times I feel inadequate and know I can do nothing without you, yet in and through Your name I have so much to give and can do anything you ask of me. Please teach me and help me seek your direction so that I know what you want me to give and where you want me to give it. Amen.

14 NOVEMBER

Obey God, Not Men

Acts 5 v 29: Peter and the other apostles replied: "We must obey God rather than men!"

Peter and the apostles have been brought before the Jewish leaders and told not to speak in Jesus' name anymore, but Peter makes it quite clear where they all stand. They will not bow down to what men tell them to do but will continue to follow wholeheartedly whatever God tells them to do. This should be the same for us whenever we are tempted to buckle under peer pressure, or any other type of pressure that would try to lure us away from following what God has shown us to do.

Peter and the apostles loved God even more than their own lives. They were one hundred per cent committed to Jesus and his call on their lives; no matter what, they would always obey God before men! How about you?

O Lord, please toughen me up, so that I can take my stand against all those who would try to deter me from carrying out your will, even if it costs me dearly. I ask you to strengthen me, even now, in Jesus' precious name. Amen.

15 NOVEMBER

Seen the Light!

Acts 9 v 18: Immediately, something like scales fell from Saul's eyes, and he could see again. He got up and was baptized...

Previous to this, Saul has met with the risen Lord Jesus and been blinded by the brightness of the light all around him. Now three days later, as directed by Jesus, he has been prayed for to see again and to be filled with the Holy Spirit. Saul had most certainly seen the light, because as soon as his sight returns he gets baptised straight away - no questions asked!

This has made me wonder if we sometimes go around with scales on our eyes, not being able to see what God is really doing. Maybe we need someone to come and pray for us, to help us to get rid of our blind spots? Once Saul can see, there is no hesitation – he wants to be baptised. I wonder why we so often put off being baptised. Is it, I wonder, because we haven't truly seen the light?

O Heavenly Father, please remove any scales that may be covering my eyes and preventing me from seeing you and your will for my life. I am willing for you to send someone to pray for me if that's what it takes. Amen.

16 NOVEMBER

Oh What a Witness!

Acts 16 v 25: About midnight Paul and Silas were praying and singing hymns to God, and the other prisoners were listening to them.

The story that follows this verse is just amazing and well worth a read, but what is astonishing about the verse is that even while in agony and in chains, Paul and Silas are still putting God and his kingdom before their own needs. They are choosing to praise God instead of complaining about their circumstances - what a witness to their fellow prisoners! Ouch - I think I know what I would've been doing in their situation, how about you?

Time and time again we see in the scriptures how powerful praise is, especially when it is a real sacrifice! I firmly believe that if Paul and Silas had just spent their time moaning and complaining and feeling sorry for themselves then nothing amazing would've happened that night. I wonder how many miracles we are missing out on because we don't praise our God in our darkest times.

Dear Lord, I put my hand up here and confess that I find it much easier to grumble and complain my way through tough times rather than turning to you in prayer and praise. Thank you for showing me this today, please help me to change.
Amen.

17 NOVEMBER

For Your Whole Family

Acts 16 v 34: The jailer brought them into his house and set a meal before them; he was filled with joy because he had come to believe in God – he and his whole family.

Following Paul and Silas singing praises to God, there is a large earthquake and the doors of the jail fly open and everyone's chains come loose! The terrified jailer asks how he can be saved and they tell him to believe in the Lord Jesus and he and his whole household will be saved!

As we have seen before, God often chooses to save a whole household, rather than just an individual. It shows just how important families are to Him, that he cares for our loved ones as much as he does for us and how he longs for all of them to be saved. May this encourage you to never give up praying for your family members that don't yet know Jesus as their Lord and Saviour.

O Father, I thank you that you love my family even more than I do. I cry out to you for all those in my family that don't yet know you or your Son Jesus. Please draw them to yourself by the power of your Holy Spirit. In Jesus' name I ask this.
Amen.

18 NOVEMBER

Compelled by the Spirit

Acts 20 v 22: And now, compelled by the Spirit, I am going to Jerusalem, not knowing what will happen to me there.

I guess the question is, 'How did the Holy Spirit compel Paul to go to Jerusalem?' As the Holy Spirit lives within us, I am sure Paul had a strong inner sense that he must go there, and in the following verse he tells us that he has been warned by the Holy Spirit that prison and hardships await him. Just like Jesus, Paul doesn't flinch from any of it, but resolutely sets out for Jerusalem, just as Jesus did.

Is there something you know God wants you to do? Or maybe somewhere he wants you to go? Have you been sensing that inner nudge from the Holy Spirit within you, but ignoring it because you really don't fancy it? May I encourage you today to be strong and courageous and to follow that inner nudge, even though you don't know what will happen to you. Once you've obeyed God you will immediately receive a deep sense of 'peace' but sadly, only turmoil within if you continue to ignore it.

Thank you Lord for encouraging me to step out into what you have asked of me. Please forgive me for not wanting to – I choose now to trust you with it all. Amen.

19 NOVEMBER

Shake Him Off

Acts 28 v 5: But Paul shook the snake off into the fire and suffered no ill effects.

What a picture this paints of Satan's ultimate end. Although he may do his utmost to try and take us out by latching on to us, we are under our Lord's protection, and in the end he will be thrown into the fiery furnace.

When evil tries to attach itself onto you, there is only one thing to do with it and that is shake it off! The enemy may even come in the subtle guise of a friend trying to help you, like when Peter told Jesus he wasn't to suffer and die (see Matthew 16 v 21-23). As long as we are following Jesus we will face challenges and temptations along the way, which Satan will use to try to immobilise us and keep us from carrying out God's will. But take heart, Jesus covers you with his protection; He will keep you safe from harm, just as he protected Paul from any harmful effects from the snake!

O Lord Jesus, you know exactly what it's like to be tempted by Satan and in the end you said, 'Away from me Satan!' and, praise God, he left you! Please help me to shake him off as soon as I sense there is even a hint of evil going on. Amen.

20 NOVEMBER

Love like No Other

Romans 5 v 8: But God demonstrates his own love for us in this: While we were still sinners, Christ died for us.

'While we were still sinners' - this is when God gave everything he had for us; not when we started to believe in him, nor when we started to live to please him – it was when we were still hostile towards him and still living to please ourselves! Has anyone else ever loved you in this way? Now spend a moment meditating on what all this means to you personally.

God loves you in a way that is beyond tracing out, beyond understanding. He saw you in your mess and he loved you – just as you were! He wanted to have a relationship with you, so showed the full extent of his love for you by allowing his one and only Son to die the most torturous of deaths, to win your love and have you by his side forever! Where else will you find such love?

O Father God, when I really stop and think about what you have done for me, it cuts right to my heart. Words can never explain what I feel inside, how 'blown away' I am by the knowledge of just how much you love me. Please help me to fully grasp it - and then receive it, in Jesus' precious name.
Amen.

21 NOVEMBER

No More Fear

Romans 8 v 15: For you did not receive a spirit that makes you a slave again to fear, but you received the Spirit of sonship. And by him we cry, "Abba, Father."

If God is our Father – he who created the heavens and the earth and who sits enthroned above it all - why would we ever be afraid? If we have the creator of the universe on our side, looking out for us all the time, what could we possibly worry about? And yet fear and worry we do!

Next time fear comes knocking at your door, stand firm in your faith and trust in your heavenly Father's love and care for you. He will not allow anything to happen to you that is not a part of his perfect will and plan for your life, as long as you are following him and his ways. If you can really grasp this fact it will dispel all fear from within you! So cast off that spirit of fear, for it no longer belongs in you; you are a Child of God!

O my Heavenly Father, how foolish I am at times, allowing myself to be filled with doubts and fear, when all the time you are right there, watching over me, protecting me completely and in control of every situation in my life. Please forgive my distrust. I tell all fear to 'Go now, in Jesus' name!' Amen.

22 NOVEMBER

Beautiful Feet

Romans 10 v 15: And how can they preach unless they are sent? As it is written, "How beautiful are the feet of those who bring good news!"

We were never meant to keep all this good news to ourselves. It was always made for sharing, and God wants to make use of your 'beautiful feet' to carry His message to those who have never heard about what Jesus has done for them, through dying on the cross.

Yes, God is sending you! You have his Word in your heart and in your mouth and now you need to 'Go' and spread the good news wherever and to whoever you can! Wherever God may send you!

We all have this good news to share, and it does need sharing. Step out in faith, even today and start telling the good news about Jesus!

O Lord, this feels very challenging to me and yet, at the same time some excitement is stirring within. May my feet be willing to go where you send me and my mouth willing to speak what you tell me; in Jesus' name. Amen.

23 NOVEMBER

Love One Another

Romans 12 v 10: Be devoted to one another in brotherly love. Honour one another above yourselves.

True love does no harm to his neighbour and puts his neighbour's needs before his own. There is no room for comparing and jealousy and yet we find it so hard to love like this – I know I do!

As Christians we should look different to the rest of the world; our love for one another should be so outstanding that others are drawn to the Lord because of it. Jesus himself said 'By this all men will know that you are my disciples, if you love one another.' This commandment is really important to God, second only to us loving God with all our heart. As we are out there representing God, people are watching us far more than we may realise, and they can see right through any phoniness!

Thank you Lord Jesus for showing us just how important it is to love our brothers and sisters. Our love should far outshine this world's version of love, but I confess I so often fail at this. Lord, I really need your help here – please! Amen.

24 NOVEMBER

United We Stand

Romans 15 v 5: May the God who gives endurance and encouragement give you a spirit of unity among yourselves as you follow Christ Jesus...

As the saying goes, 'united we stand, divided we fall' - this is so true and our enemy knows it. This is why one of the chief aims of Satan is to cause division wherever he can, and can't we just see his work everywhere we look in the world today! His aim is to pull us down, and destroy us. Whenever we join in with any quarrelling or disputes we are actually helping him!

Today's verse is so encouraging, as it tells us how! How can we keep this unity between us? By asking God to give us a spirit of unity! It was never meant to come about by our own human effort, so it's no wonder that we often fail. All we need to do is confess we cannot do it ourselves and ask God to do what only he can do!

Thank you for your word Lord, thank you for showing us the way to live in unity. I ask you today to give us a spirit of unity, not only among us, but amongst all your believers worldwide. Amen.

25 NOVEMBER

Weak Made Strong

1 Corinthians 1 v 27: But God chose the foolish things of the world to shame the wise; God chose the weak things of the world to shame the strong.

When God came to this earth, he didn't choose to be born into a royal household even though he was a king, and he didn't choose to show himself to be rich and famous even though he owned the whole world. No, he chose instead, to be born in a stable and for lowly shepherds to be his first visitors! How humbling is that!

God's heart is for the weak, for when we are weak we can then become strong in and through Him! This way God gets all the glory and the strong are left in awe of God's power, as it is made known through the weak. I would far rather be weak, fully relying on God, than think I am strong and then find I cannot cope. How about you?

Dear God, I just love the way you turn this world's values upside down; you make the strong weak and the weak strong! And the wise foolish and the foolish wise – you are awesome and I adore you. May I be weak and foolish for You! Amen.

26 NOVEMBER

Run to Get the Prize

1 Corinthians 9 v 24: Do you not know that in a race all the runners run, but only one gets the prize? Run in such a way as to get the prize.

What is Paul saying here? Surely he is not suggesting that only one person will get to heaven? No, of course he isn't, but there is a very strong message here for us which is so easy to miss if we just read this verse quickly!

What Paul is saying here is that we need to be one hundred per cent committed to following Jesus, no half measures. Just as an athlete, who is passionate about winning a race, trains in preparation and puts every effort into it – so must we as we follow Jesus. We need to take our life with Jesus seriously and give him everything we have. I know this is a challenging word today, but it is something we need to hear.

O Lord, I confess that all too often I take the easy way, the lazy route, rather than giving my best to you. Please forgive me. Wake me up today, Lord, that I may be inspired to press on and give you my all. May my sole aim be to win the race! Amen.

27 NOVEMBER

Way Out

1 Corinthians 10 v 13: No temptation has seized you except what is common to man. And God is faithful; he will not let you be tempted beyond what you can bear. But when you are tempted, he will also provide a way out so that you can stand up under it.

We all get tempted at times, and in many different ways. If I'm honest, when I hear the word 'temptation' I tend to think of sexual temptation first, but it can equally apply to the temptation to gossip, to lie, to lose your temper, to eat or drink too much, to please yourself before others - the list goes on.

God promises we won't be tempted beyond what we can bear, which means we should always be able to control ourselves in whichever area we have the problem. Temptation itself isn't a sin; it's the giving in to it that is, and yet God promises us a 'way out' of any such temptation. Perhaps next time you are tempted, rather than striving not to fall into it, look for the 'way out' that God is providing for you. For example, if you are tempted to gossip about someone, the 'way out' could be to speak well of them instead.

Thank you Lord for providing a 'way out'; please help me to look for it each time I am being tempted. Amen.

28 NOVEMBER

Love Is the Key

1 Corinthians 13 v 2: If I have the gift of prophecy and can fathom all mysteries and all knowledge, and if I have a faith that can move mountains, but have not love, I am nothing.

Love is the key to the kingdom of God; without it we are still lost and remain outside. Our motives must be genuine, kind and loving when we do anything for the Lord, because he is never fooled by our outward show of 'good works'. God is always interested in our hearts, for it is there that true love resides.

We may do the most amazing things for God, even great miracles, but if we have no love in our hearts then God sees all we do as straw, ready to be burnt up. It is so easy, once we are being used by God, to fall into the trap of thinking that 'we' are doing it, and it can so easily become about 'me' and 'my' ministry. But it should always be about God, and our love for him and others should always be the motivating factor. What a warning this is to us.

O Lord, please don't let my heart grow cold, may 'love' always be the motive in all I do for You. Amen.

29 NOVEMBER
Bring and Share

1 Corinthians 14 v 26: ... When you come together, everyone has a hymn, or a word of instruction, a revelation, a tongue or an interpretation. All of these must be done for the strengthening of the church.

God gave us the various gifts of the Spirit, not to show off our spiritual prowess, but so that we could bless one another by using them, as we are led by his Spirit. As we gather together to worship, we come first and foremost to pour out our love and adoration to God, but we also come to receive from Him, to hear what he wants to say to us. He does this by speaking to us by his Spirit, whether it is through a hymn, a sermon, a prophecy, a scripture reading or through another tongue with an interpretation. All this is for our mutual edification and strengthening.

We have different gifts, but they all come from the same Spirit and he gives them to each as he sees fit. So next time you feel the prompting to share something – be bold and step out, so that others may be blessed!

O Lord God, may I be far more willing to share things with my fellow believers, to help build them up and encourage them, not only during a worship service, but anytime, day or night! Amen.

30 NOVEMBER

Double Comfort

2 Corinthians 1 v 4: ... who comforts us in all our troubles, so that we can comfort those in any trouble with the comfort we ourselves have received from God.

Have you ever wondered why you have to go through so many trials in this life? I well remember, during such a trial, someone sharing today's verse with me. I found it comforting on two counts – first that God cared enough about me to be interested in my problem, so much so that he wanted to comfort me in it. Secondly, I could now understand someone else who was having, or had experienced the same situation and I would be able to share with them the comfort I had received from the Lord.

So maybe we should view all life's trials as opportunities to receive love and comfort from our heavenly Father and opportunities to share that love and comfort with others! Is there someone you could bring comfort to today?

Thank you Lord, that you are the God who comforts us in all our troubles. I receive your comfort right now Lord, and ask that you may draw me to others, who also need a special touch from you. Amen.

01 DECEMBER

Now Is the Time!

2 Corinthians 6 v 2: For he says, "In the time of my favour I heard you, and in the day of salvation I helped you." I tell you, now is the time of God's favour, now is the day of salvation.

Have you recently been crying out to God in prayer? Are you desperate to hear from Him? Do you need his help today? I sense that many of you have been weighed down by huge burdens, and you are longing for God to intervene. You have been crying out to him for help, for what seems like an age. Take heart, this verse is for you today; in fact, I am hoping that as soon as you read it you felt its personal impact. God wants to do something outstanding in your life today.

Maybe there is someone reading this who doesn't yet know Jesus as their personal Saviour, so if that is you, and you would like him to be – then today is the day of your salvation! The following prayer is for you to pray, and once you have prayed it, do let another Christian know so that they can help and encourage you further!

Thank you God for sending Jesus to die on the cross for me. Today I choose to turn away from everything that I know to be wrong and follow you Lord Jesus. Please fill me now with your Holy Spirit. Amen.

02 DECEMBER

Unequally Yoked?

2 Corinthians 6 v 14: Do not be yoked together with unbelievers. For what do righteousness and wickedness have in common? Or what fellowship can light have with darkness?

When I was a young Christian I always wondered why people advised me not to marry a non-Christian. I couldn't see it in the bible, because I didn't really understand what being 'unequally yoked' meant. Now I know better and wish others did too, because it can save a lot of needless pain and stress, and in some cases even financial ruin. Not only does this 'yoking' refer to marriage, but it can also refer to business partnerships and possibly even friendships in which we allow ourselves to be controlled by them.

When we are yoked, we are bound to the other person. Have a think about your own life now and ask the Lord to show you if you are yoked to any unbelievers. Obviously if you are married to one, God won't be telling you to leave, but in relation to business partners or close friendships it would be well worth asking his advice.

Thank you Lord, for speaking to me so clearly today; please show me if there is anything I need to do. Amen.

03 DECEMBER

Battle of Thoughts

2 Corinthians 10 v 5: We demolish arguments and every pretension that sets itself up against the knowledge of God, and we take captive every thought to make it obedient to Christ.

Where do our doubts about God and his goodness originate? Do they not come from those 'thoughts' that pop into our mind? Where does the idea to give in to temptation come from? Once again it arises initially from our thoughts. But we don't have to sit back and just let these random thoughts control our lives. No, we need to take them captive and make them line up with what we read in God's Word. Any thoughts that go against what we know to be true need to be cast out. A very good thing to do next is to purposefully think about something positive in God's word and meditate on it.

We can control our thoughts if we want to; we don't have to let them lead us into a further maze of thoughts which then distract us from our relationship with God.

Father God, thank you that I can choose my own thoughts. Please help me to remember this whenever they come thick and fast without my invitation and may I take them all captive and make them obedient to Jesus. Amen.

04 DECEMBER

True Freedom

Galatians 5 v 1: It is for freedom that Christ has set us free. Stand firm, then, and do not let yourselves be burdened again by a yoke of slavery.

In order for the Jews to be right with God, they needed to follow the law, with all its rules and regulations but, when Jesus died on the cross he did away with all that, as the way to God was then, and still is, through faith in his Son Jesus.

Why do we still want to follow rules and regulations? Why, when Jesus has paid the price for us to be free from the law, do we still try and earn our way into his affection?

Today, choose to live in the 'freedom' that Jesus died to bring you. Your relationship with him is what matters, not how many chapters of the Bible you read yesterday or how many hours you prayed today – he wants 'you'!

Please forgive me Jesus, for those times I have ignored the price you paid for my freedom; forgive me for trying to earn your love. Set me free Lord to live as you intended, in a close and personal relationship with you. Amen.

05 DECEMBER

My Full Armour

Ephesians 6 v 11: Put on the full armour of God so that you can take your stand against the devil's schemes.

One day as I read through the list of armour that we are told to put on (see verses 14 – 17), I realised that each piece was actually 'Jesus' – He is 'the truth' and 'our righteousness', He is 'the gospel of peace', He is our 'shield of faith' and 'our salvation' and He is 'the word of God'. This came as such a relief to me, as I struggled to remember each piece by name. Now all I needed to do was to make sure I had 'put on Jesus', so to speak, for He is my full armour!

If we are unsure that we are saved, the devil will cause us to doubt it even more and we will become anxious. Likewise, if we don't believe we are righteous through Jesus, he can easily fill us with bad thoughts about ourselves and we will feel far from God and discouraged. Those are just two examples of how not wearing our armour gives the devil a way in and why we need it on every day!

Thank you Lord Jesus, You are all I need in order to take my stand against the devil's schemes. May I live, totally trusting in you every day of my life. Amen.

06 DECEMBER

Give it Up!

Philippians 4 v 6: Do not be anxious about anything, but in everything, by prayer and petition, with thanksgiving, present your requests to God.

Feeling anxious and upset is not how God intends us to live. He wants us to feel comfortable enough to hand over any concerns we may have, straight to him in prayer, before we have a chance to start fretting or worrying about them. In fact, the verse following this one tells us what the result will be if we do this – God's peace will come and guard both our hearts and minds from anxiety. And just in case you are wondering - yes, this really does work, so long as you truly hand everything over to him and don't start grabbing it back and worrying again!

Is there anything that you need to hand over to the Lord in prayer? Is there anything troubling you, that's causing you anxiety? Why wait any longer when you can pray and receive his peace right now?

O Lord, please forgive me for not coming to you sooner with this. I bring it all to you now Father God; everything that is troubling me you already know! Please will you sort it out; I can't – forgive me for trying. I choose to let it all go now, in Jesus' name, and to receive your peace. Amen.

07 DECEMBER

All for Jesus

Colossians 3 v 17: And whatever you do, whether in word or deed, do it all in the name of the Lord Jesus, giving thanks to God the Father through him.

I don't know about you, but not many of my days are filled with great and exciting things to do – or are they? In fact, if I choose to take today's verse seriously, as I should, then the opposite is surely true, isn't it? Every day is filled with the excitement of living and working for Jesus. Yes, even doing mundane jobs like washing up can become a joy as you do it to please Him! If we truly take this verse to heart it will transform our lowly everyday lives into days of royal service!

Next time you are tempted to moan and groan about how boring your day is, why not turn to this verse and meditate on it, or maybe even write it out and place it where you can see it each morning?

What a privilege we have Lord, to be able to do everything we do in your precious name. Stir us up each day as we start to work for You; may we see our days ahead as exciting rather than monotonous. Amen.

08 DECEMBER

Thankful in All Situations

1 Thessalonians 5 v 18: ... give thanks in all circumstances, for this is God's will for you in Christ Jesus.

How can I be thankful when something terrible is happening I sense you ask? I totally agree; this appears very difficult, if not impossible, at first. However, if we take our eyes off the circumstances for a moment, and allow ourselves to look to Jesus, we can always praise him for who he is and all he has done for us. If we truly believe that God works 'all' things together for our good, then surely it follows that whatever is happening to us, and however bad it gets, we know it has an ultimate purpose for our, or someone else's good, and therefore we can give thanks!

So not only should we be thankful during the trial, but we can reach a point where we are thankful for it, because of all the 'good' that will finally result from it, even though we may not get to see it for a while.

Dear Heavenly Father, please remind me next time I am in a dark place, not to resort to grumbling and complaining about it, but instead to turn it into an opportunity to thank and praise you. Amen.

09 DECEMBER

Fear No Evil

2 Thessalonians 3 v 3: But the Lord is faithful, and he will strengthen and protect you from the evil one.

One of the last prayers Jesus prayed with his disciples, before he was arrested in the garden, was that after he had gone, God would protect them from the evil one. Now we may have doubts that God will answer some of our prayers, but surely there can be no doubt that God will answer the prayer of his own dear Son!

Today's verse is yet another confirmation that we are being protected from the devil by God himself. If we truly believe this, we will no longer live in fear of evil because when you really get down to it, fear is a result of us not fully trusting or believing that God has us safely covered, that he is always watching over us and strengthening us for whatever lays ahead. So, if fear is something that has plagued you, I encourage you today, to break off its chains by fully believing that God has you covered!

Thank you Lord for revealing this 'truth' to me today and in such a powerful way! Fear may come knocking, but I am going to refuse it entry and choose instead to trust in my heavenly Father's protection. Amen.

10 DECEMBER

Open Your Gift!

1 Timothy 4 v 14: Do not neglect your gift, which was given you through a prophetic message when the body of elders laid their hands on you.

Let's imagine, you desperately need a new coffee maker; you do a lot of entertaining and people expect nice coffee when they come to your house. It is almost Christmas Day and you are pretty sure that one of the presents under the tree is, in fact, a new coffee maker – but you can't use it while it is still wrapped up under the tree!

This may seem a rather silly illustration but I hope it gets the point across - while that gift lays unopened under the tree it is of no use to anyone! No one gets the benefit of what that gift can bring. Not only are you deprived but so are all those that come to your house for coffee!

My question to you today is – 'What gifts do you have that are still lying unopened, under the tree?' Maybe it is time to dust them off and open them up, so that others may be blessed by what God has given you?

Dear Lord, please forgive me for not using the gifts you've given me, which, in turn, has caused others to miss out on your blessings. I choose today to take off the wrapping! Amen.

11 DECEMBER

Too Shy?

2 Timothy 1 v 7: For God did not give us a spirit of timidity, but a spirit of power, of love and of self-discipline.

Some of us are naturally more timid than others so will have a much bigger struggle in this area, but there are times in all our lives when we may well feel rather small and not quite so sure of ourselves – especially when we encounter the unfamiliar.

Timothy was naturally timid, and so Paul reminds him here that God doesn't want us to be timid, but bold. God has given us a spirit of power and when motivated by a spirit of love, we can discipline ourselves to step out from the shadows and be bold for God, using the gifts he has given us.

If you struggle in this way, I encourage you to ask God to fill you afresh each day with His Holy Spirit, knowing that everything you do will be made that much easier, relying on His power, rather than looking to your own.

O Lord, I really struggle with shyness, and I so want to be bold for you. Please fill me with your Holy Spirit and enable me to come out of the shadows for you. Amen.

12 DECEMBER

Don't Argue!

Titus 3 v 9: But avoid foolish controversies and genealogies and arguments and quarrels about the law, because these are unprofitable and useless.

Isn't it so easy to fall into the enticement to argue? All arguments really stem from 'pride' – the belief that we are right and everyone else is wrong - we know best! I wonder how many churches have split, how many marriages ended in divorce or friendships broken up just because of stupid arguments? It is quite sobering to think about really, and it's all because our stupid pride won't allow us to just stay quiet, admit that we were wrong, or say we are sorry!

We are warned not to argue, several times in God's word, but why do we find it so hard not to? If we valued others and their opinions above our own, then we would be far less likely to argue with them. For example, who would have dared argue with our late Queen – Elizabeth II? Most people wouldn't have, because they valued her above themselves; and that's how we should value everyone! Then we will stop arguing!

O Lord, please have mercy! Forgive my foolish pride, for thinking I always know best! Humble me I pray, that I may honour others above myself. Amen.

13 DECEMBER

Shared Blessing

Philemon v 6: I pray that you may be active in sharing your faith, so that you will have a full understanding of every good thing we have in Christ.

I expect you find that, like me, today's verse is not overly familiar to you and is easy to read quickly so that you miss what it is saying. At first I thought it was just an encouragement to share our faith with others, which is brilliant in itself, but as I looked closer I realised it was showing us why we should do this and the answer rather surprised me!

As we share our faith with others, we need to be familiar with what we believe, in other words, the full gospel. As a result we are constantly being reminded of all the good things that we have in Christ and all we have to look forward to in the next life, so not only do we bless those with whom we share our faith, but we also bless ourselves! What great motivation to share our faith, in whichever way we can!

Thank you Heavenly Father, for showing me the many rewards of sharing my faith with others; please may I become more active in doing this and, as I do so, become fully aware of all that I have in You! Amen.

14 DECEMBER

In Our Shoes

Hebrews 2 v 18: Because he himself suffered when he was tempted, he is able to help those who are being tempted.

Jesus has walked 'in our shoes'; he has experienced intense temptation. He is human like us and knows how we feel when being tempted, so because he has been where we have, He is there to help us in our hour of need, for he has promised never to leave us!

Next time you feel you can no longer resist temptation, remember that Jesus has suffered in the same way as you and understands exactly what you are going through right now. May this bring you comfort and hope that there is a way out for you! Cry out to Jesus to come and help you resist, and stand firm against the wiles of the enemy.

O Lord Jesus, it is so comforting to know that you have walked in my shoes; you know exactly what this temptation feels like. Please help me to resist, and strengthen me to get through this trial. In your precious name I ask it. Amen.

15 DECEMBER

The Power of God's Word

Hebrews 4 v 12: For the word of God is living and active. Sharper than any double-edged sword, it penetrates even to dividing soul and spirit, joints and marrow; it judges the thoughts and attitudes of the heart.

No wonder our enemy doesn't want us reading God's word – he knows the power it contains - and he definitely doesn't want us speaking it out loud as it's sure to send him packing! This is exactly what Jesus did when he was tempted by Satan in the wilderness and it is exactly what we should do too! There is Power in God's Word!

As we read the Bible, it has the ability to bring us peace, to heal us and set us free from addictions, to challenge us to forgive someone that has hurt us and to reveal to us where we are going wrong, showing us the things we need to change or put right in our lives. Let us embrace all that God wants to do with His Word!

Dear Lord, thank you so much for Your Word; may I never forget the power and authority that is held within it's pages. May I use it wisely to defeat the enemy and to grow in my Christian faith and walk with you. Amen.

16 DECEMBER

Faith's Reward

Hebrews 11 v 6: And without faith it is impossible to please God, because anyone who comes to him must believe that he exists and that he rewards those who earnestly seek him.

Could this possibly be what is at the root of a lot of our problems? We don't really believe that God will reward us when we seek him? In other words, we don't have faith in God's good character; we doubt that he really wants to be good to us. And yet, it clearly says here in Hebrews, that in order to please God we need to believe this!

One of the main reasons we often fail to take hold of God's blessings is our sense of not being worthy of His love. Who do we think we are to receive his many rewards? But what a revelation – this actually displeases God! So accept this word for you today – God longs to reward you whenever you seek Him!

O Lord, this has been a real 'wake up' call for me today. Please forgive me for the times I haven't believed in your ultimate goodness towards me or that you have wanted to reward me. I choose to believe that you will reward me, as I earnestly seek you. Amen.

17 DECEMBER

Fix Your Eyes on Jesus

Hebrews 12 v 2: Let us fix our eyes on Jesus, the author and perfecter of our faith, who for the joy set before him endured the cross, scorning its shame, and sat down at the right hand of the throne of God.

If we trust in our own ability to get us through things we will soon flounder; if we concentrate on the problems that surround us we will begin to sink – just as Peter did when he walked on the water and took his eyes off of Jesus and looked at the waves instead!

We need to fix our eyes on Jesus, because he has been there and has the answers. If we look to Jesus, he shows us how to deal with our tough situations. He shows us to look ahead to our future reward and to trust in God to get us through the trials we face, because that is exactly what he did. And so we must not lose heart when we are up against it, however loudly the storm is raging around us. If we keep our focus on Jesus, we are more than able to get through this!

O Lord Jesus, it is so easy to lose sight of you when I am going through such hard times; when the storm is screaming so loudly in my ears that it is all I am aware of – but I need to look to You. Please remind me of this. Amen.

18 DECEMBER

Confess and be Blessed

James 5 v 16: Therefore confess your sins to each other and pray for each other so that you may be healed. The prayer of a righteous man is powerful and effective.

As I read this verse, I realised that we tend to focus on the second part - about the prayer of a righteous man being effective - which is a good thing, and yet we seem to gloss over the first part where we are told to confess our sins to each other – 'ouch!' Have you ever heard a sermon on this or been told to actively do this in church? My guess is that the answer for most of you is 'No!' Could this possibly be one of the reasons why so many of us are unwell?

This is very challenging, I agree, and yet I can't help but feel rather excited! Just think of all the possibilities if we actually did this. I believe we would see many more healings taking place amongst us, and a new level of peace and freedom in our lives. It would be a great leveller too as we realise that we all fall short! No room for any pride here!

O Heavenly Father, thank you so much for revealing this hidden gem among the pages of your word. May I be willing to share this with others and find someone I can actually do this with in my own life. Amen.

19 DECEMBER
Be Considerate

1 Peter 3 v 15: ... Always be prepared to give an answer to everyone who asks you to give the reason for the hope that you have. But do this with gentleness and respect...

Sometimes in our excitement or eagerness we may start sharing our faith in a way that makes the person we are sharing it with feel small or overwhelmed, or even trapped. This is why we need to do it gently and with respect for the other person.

Sadly, my own father was put off by some rather over-zealous Christians who tried to get him 'saved' while on a boat. My poor father felt completely trapped and was so traumatised by the event that it kept him constricted in his own narrow religious life, and therefore prevented him from ever knowing the fullness and freedom of a life with Jesus. This is not only sad, but devastating, and it hurts the heart of our God. I believe this story serves as a reminder to us of the great power God has invested in us and how we need to use it wisely.

Please help me, Father, to share my faith, while giving full consideration to the person I am speaking to. In my eagerness, help me to show both gentleness and respect.
Amen.

20 DECEMBER

God's Patience

2 Peter 3 v 9: The Lord is not slow in keeping his promise, as some understand slowness. He is patient with you, not wanting anyone to perish, but everyone to come to repentance.

Here we see that God's heart is for the lost – there is no-one he doesn't want to save! So never doubt if it is God's will to pray for someone's salvation, it most definitely is, but he will never force himself on anyone. He cannot over-ride a person's free will, for that is the gift he has given to us all.

If God is so patient with the lost, then so should we be. It may take years of friendship with someone before they respond to the things you have shared with them over those years, and if God is patient, then who are we to give up on someone. Be encouraged today if you are praying for a lost soul. Their salvation may be nearer than you think – never give up on them; for God never gave up on you!

Thank you Lord for your infinite patience. You have never given up on me, so please help me to be just as patient as I pray for those who don't yet know you - in Jesus' name. Amen.

21 DECEMBER

I Am a Child of God

1 John 3 v 1: How great is the love the Father has lavished on us, that we should be called children of God! And that is what we are!

If someone asked you today, 'Who are you?' what would be your most likely response? Most of us would probably say what our job was or that we were a mother, or a student or a pensioner, etc. These answers all say more about what we do than who we really are and sadly, they may be from where we get our worth and value - hence the phrase, 'I'm 'just' a housewife'. But if you are a believer in the Lord Jesus Christ, you are in fact a 'Child of God', and this should be your main identity; and what greater identity could you possibly have?

Try making this your first thought of the day, 'I am a Child of God!' Then repeat it to yourself several times during the day, especially when things get tough. I pretty much guarantee this will make your 'self-worth' rise to new heights, and that you will be far more aware of God's presence and his overwhelming love for you.

O Father God, thank you that you are my heavenly Father and that I am your precious child; may I live each day of my life aware of this amazing truth. Amen.

22 DECEMBER

Stay in the Word

2 John v 9: Anyone who runs ahead and does not continue in the teaching of Christ does not have God...

In the last days, there will be many false prophets, who will no longer stick to God's Word, but will instead come up with their own ideas, and so deceive many.

The best way to protect ourselves from being deceived is to stay close to Jesus and stay in his word. If people are telling you to do things that are not in agreement with the Bible, then you know they have not been sent by God. Just because something professes to be 'Christian', doesn't necessarily mean that it is. I have been to at least three 'Christian' events where the speakers were not speaking in accordance with God's Word, and the sad thing was that almost everyone went along with what they were being told to do by these people.

We will be far less likely to be taken in if we really know God's Word, which is why it is so important that we read it regularly and become familiar with it. We can use it to test whether something is of God or not!

O Lord, keep me close to you and help me to learn more of Your Word so that I can be discerning in these last days.
Amen.

23 DECEMBER

Pray a Blessing

3 John v 2: Dear friend, I pray that you may enjoy good health and that all may go well with you, even as your soul is getting along well.

We have so much to thank God for; he has made the biggest sacrifice anyone can make. He allowed his one and only Son to be tortured and killed just for us! He did this so that we could live a life of fullness in Him!

As we ourselves have received such a great blessing, let us now choose to bless others. Why not think of some people you know and pray this verse as a blessing over them today. In fact, pray it often over them and then watch and be amazed at the changes God will bring about in their lives.

God wants us to be well in spirit, body and soul; he is interested in every part of us. Now receive this prayer of blessing for yourself and pray it over your family.

Thank you Lord for all you have done for me. Since you have blessed me so much, may I now bless others by praying today's verse over them; please bring people into my mind as I pray. Amen.

24 DECEMBER

He Is Able

Jude v 24: To him who is able to keep you from falling and to present you before his glorious presence without fault and with great joy...

If you have ever had one of those days when you feel you've failed the Lord yet again and are wondering if you will ever get it right, or be good enough to get into heaven, then this verse is a good one to turn to. And if today is one of those days – then God is so speaking to you right now!

It is no longer about us getting it right or being 'good' enough, that is the old covenant. Jesus took all our wrong-doing on the cross and has given us His own righteousness, so that we are now seen as 'faultless' by God. I know it is unbelievable when you really stop and think about it, but it is true! This is why we should be so full of 'joy' each day, knowing that God is more than able to keep us from falling and confident we will one day be in his glorious presence forever!

Dear Heavenly Father, just reading today's verse has sent shivers of joy running through me and to realise that you see me as faultless, despite my many failings, is just too good for words. Thank you! Amen.

25 DECEMBER

Love Re-kindled

Revelation 2 v 4: Yet I hold this against you: You have forsaken your first love.

The Risen Lord Jesus spoke these words to a church that was hard working, persevering and even facing hardships for His name, but sadly they had lost their first love for Him! This is such an important word for us; we may be doing all the right things, but if we are neglecting our relationship with Jesus then we need help!

It is so easy to take a relationship for granted. We lose that first excitement and joy of getting to know someone. We stop giving them our full attention and spend less quality time with them, and this can easily be true of our relationship with Jesus too! We need to re-kindle our first love for Jesus; we need to do the things we did when we first came to know him as our Lord and Saviour!

Will you give Jesus your whole heart afresh today? And will you continue to do so for all of your days?

Thank you Lord Jesus, that you love me so much that you desire my love for you to remain as strong as it ever was. Please forgive me for allowing it to fade and for relying on my good deeds. I love you Lord! Amen.

26 DECEMBER

Open Door

Revelation 3 v 8: I know your deeds. See, I have placed before you an open door that no-one can shut. I know that you have little strength, yet you have kept my word and have not denied my name.

It is such a powerful encouragement to realise that the Lord knows all that we do for him, he sees everything; yes, even our struggles and weaknesses. Be encouraged today if you are feeling weak; God fully understands and he loves you no less for it.

God is telling some of you today that he has placed before you an open door and to others, who already have that door in front of them, he is saying that you don't need to fear it closing, as no-one can shut it! So take heart, however tough things may look. God is opening up a new way of opportunity for you and no enemy can thwart it!

Thank you Lord for Your Word, I so needed this encouragement today! Thank you that, despite my weaknesses, you still love me and I thank you for all the opportunities you are opening up for me; may I be willing to walk through this open door! Amen.

27 DECEMBER

Knock, Knock!

Revelation 3 v 20: Here I am! I stand at the door and knock. If anyone hears my voice and opens the door, I will come in and eat with him, and he with me.

Jesus speaks these words to a church that has become 'lukewarm' in their faith and love; he is urging them to repent. He is right there knocking at the door to their hearts! Can you hear him knocking at your heart today?

Jesus will never force his way into your heart or life; he does the knocking from the outside, and you will need to open the door to allow him to come in. Is he outside knocking at your door right now?

If you open the door, Jesus will come in and eat with you and you with him – you will share with each other in a most close and intimate way. Isn't it amazing that Jesus, the one and only Son of the living God, would choose to come and dine with you! But the question is - will you let Him in?

O Lord Jesus, I know you are always there, just waiting and longing to have close fellowship with me. Forgive me for not opening my door to you. Please come in now, and dine with me today! Amen.

28 DECEMBER

We Shall Overcome

Revelation 12 v 11: They overcame him by the blood of the Lamb and by the word of their testimony; they did not love their lives so much as to shrink from death.

In these last days, the enemy is going to ramp up his attacks and evil strategies against us, but we will 'overcome' him if we remain steadfast and faithful to our God. There is no need to fear death, for we have been purchased with the precious blood of Jesus. We belong to Jesus and Satan has no claim over us now! In Jesus we can overcome anything the enemy chooses to throw at us, because we know whose we are and where we are going! The enemy is powerless to stop us, for even death cannot separate us from the love of God and our ultimate destination!

We need to encourage one another all the more during these last days, as this world we live in becomes spiritually darker. We need to press into God and become a shining light to guide and save others from the darkness.

O Father God, please help me to be a good witness for you in these last days. May I even be willing to give up my own life, so that I may overcome, no matter what! Amen.

29 DECEMBER

Prepare for His Return

Revelation 16 v 15: Behold, I come like a thief! Blessed is he who stays awake and keeps his clothes with him, so that he may not go naked and be shamefully exposed.

This is one of the most exciting things about the Christian faith; we are not worshipping a dead Saviour but are awaiting his imminent return! No-one knows when he will come, except for the Father. Even Jesus doesn't know the time set for him to return. We know it will be unexpected; as he says, he'll come like a thief, and therefore we need to be ready!

How should we be prepared? I believe we need to have our robe of righteousness close at hand so that we are fully dressed to meet the Lord. We will need to have kept a short account too, asked for forgiveness for our sins and forgiven all those who have hurt us, for then we will not be ashamed when he comes! As we don't know when this will be, we need to be ready every day!

So how prepared are you right now? Are there any things you need to put right with God or others?

Thank you Lord Jesus that you are coming soon; please help me make sure I am fully prepared each day! Amen.

30 DECEMBER

Pure Wedded Bliss

Revelation 19 v 7: Let us rejoice and be glad and give him glory! For the wedding of the Lamb has come, and his bride has made herself ready.

We are the bride, can you believe it? It is true! The Church is the bride of Christ and when the bridegroom comes there will be much joy and celebration, like never before!

This is what we have been waiting for – our ultimate union with the Lord Jesus Christ. No more distractions, temptations or interruptions to our courtship – just 'pure wedded bliss' to look forward to! This is the one wedding where this phrase will be totally true! Don't you just long for that day?

He is coming for us soon, so let us rejoice and be glad. Let this give us something to look forward to during the difficult days that lay ahead.

Dear Lord Jesus, I can't wait for our 'Wedding Day'. At last we will be together and nothing will be able to come between us again! O what 'Joy' fills my heart – to think that you have chosen even me! Thank you Jesus! Amen.

31 DECEMBER

Happily Ever After

Revelation 21 v 3: And I heard a loud voice from the throne saying, "Now the dwelling of God is with men, and he will live with them. They will be his people, and God himself will be with them and be their God."

This has always been God's intention from the very beginning, that one day we would see him 'face to face' and be with him forever; no more tears, death, mourning or pain. This is one story that really does have a 'fairy tale' ending, for it can truly be said of those who follow Jesus, that one day we will all live 'happily ever after' - with Him!

God desires as many people as possible to enjoy this glorious future, and that includes you, if you would like to know Jesus as your personal saviour and friend. If this is you, then today's prayer has been written especially for you and anyone else who would like to re-commit their life to Jesus; for He is the Way, the Truth and the Life!

Dear Father God, please forgive me for all the wrong things I have thought, said or done. I choose to turn away from these now and I ask you, Lord Jesus, to come into my life and fill me with Your Holy Spirit, so I may live for You and be with You, both now and forever. Amen.

ABOUT THE AUTHOR

Carol, who currently lives in the South West of England, grew up being taken along to church each Sunday and became a Christian during her early teens. However, she always felt something was missing in her Christian life and struggled to stay on the straight and narrow path at times.

Then in the summer of 1984 she had a powerful experience of being filled with God's Holy Spirit and from that day on her life was never quite the same!

God began to teach and guide Carol in a personal way, both through his Word and the gifts of the Holy Spirit. God's Word became especially important to her and she felt passionate about reading it and learning more about her Lord.

In more recent years that passion has led to Carol wanting to share the amazing truths of God's Word with others; that they may receive all the blessings He has for them, just as she has!

Printed in Great Britain
by Amazon